PRAISE FOR HOW TO HANDLE OFFENSES

Bishop Dr. Israel Forlu, General Overseer, River of Life Assemblies Int'l. (ROLAI) USA

How to Handle Offenses is a book that every pilgrim on life's journey should read. It is essential for those seeking effective strategies to manage relationships and navigate conflicts. Dr. Mercy Forlu invested considerable time and personal sacrifice to develop this transformative work, aimed at liberating individuals from various forms of bondage. Drawing on years of teaching and divine inspiration, her profound insights have facilitated healing within numerous families and individuals. The book compellingly illustrates the power of forgiveness, even in the face of significant offenses, and highlights its profound benefits. I wholeheartedly recommend this book as it has the potential to significantly impact and enhance your life.

Julius N. Esunge, Ph.D., Fulbright Scholar, Professor, and Chair of Mathematics, President, Hope Outreach International Ministries

Dr. Mercy Forlu has hit a home run with this compelling and pragmatic discussion of a most relevant topic. Her tenderness and passion for quality relationships among humans inform her motivation in this classical discourse. Eunice and I will always be indebted to her for her wisdom in years past and this fantastic treasure she now blesses the world with.

Dr. Francis Myles, Bestselling Author: The Order of Melchizedek and Issuing Divine Restraining Orders from the Courts of Heaven

Pastor Mercy Forlu's book, *How to Handle Offenses*, is a revolutionary book on a subject that the Body of Christ desperately needs to master. The subject of offenses is one of the main areas Satan is using to cause chinks in the full armour of God that the saints are supposed to be dressed in for the day of battle. This book contains the antidote to the poison of offence that has plagued the Body of Christ and led to much damage to kingdom relationships. I highly recommend this book for every serious believer in the army of God.

Rev. Dr. Kenneth Tah, Superintendent, US Full Gospel Mission Fellowship

In a world marred by misunderstandings, conflicts, and emotional wounds, Dr. Mercy Forlu's book, *How to Handle Offenses: Grace to Manifest the Power of Forgiveness*, emerges as a crucial manual for navigating the choppy waters of human relationships. With unparalleled wisdom and profound insight, Dr. Forlu tackles the multifaceted nature of offenses and the transformative power of forgiveness. Starting with the premise that "Offenses Must Come," Dr. Forlu offers profound insights and practical strategies to navigate offenses and embrace forgiveness. Chapters like "Taking Offense is a Choice" and "Offense Has Weight and Power" shed light on personal responsibility and the heavy burden of holding onto grudges. Her candid discussion on the repercussions of unforgiveness and heartening strategies for reconciliation provide valuable tools for transformation. With real-life scenarios, biblical references, and practical advice, chapters such as "How to Handle Offenses," "Ways to Avoid Being Easily Offended," and "Manifest the Power of Forgiveness" equip readers with the grace needed to forgive. The book culminates with a reminder of our shared human fallibility, "What About the Offender?" and wisdom for peaceful living in the final chapter. Dr. Forlu's work transcends mere advice, offering timeless teachings for emotional liberation, spiritual growth, and harmonious relationships. *How to Handle Offenses* is not just a guide but a transformative companion, leading readers on a journey toward forgiveness and peaceful living. Prepare to be enlightened, challenged, and profoundly transformed by the wisdom imparted in this remarkable book. Your path to emotional freedom and harmonious relationships begins here.

Rev. Gaius Forlu, Vice Overseer, River of Life Assemblies Int'l (ROLAI), San Antonio, USA

I enthusiastically endorse my mother, Dr. Mercy Forlu's, transformative book on handling offenses and embracing forgiveness. In a world where words and actions often lead to deep wounds, Dr. Forlu offers hope and practical wisdom. Her book explores the dynamics of offenses, whether intentional or unintentional. She guides readers through the healing power of forgiveness, blending psychological insight with spiritual wisdom for a holistic approach. Dr. Forlu's work reflects her expertise and compassion. She navigates the complexities of forgiveness, emphasizing its role in freeing oneself from resentment. Her practical advice and relatable stories make forgiveness accessible to all. This book is a valuable resource for anyone seeking inner peace and healthier relationships. I wholeheartedly recommend it to those who have experienced hurt or offense, as it offers a path to healing and renewed strength through forgiveness and grace.

Rev. Lenita Reeves, Overseer, Action Chapel Baltimore and Action Chapel North Carolina Churches, Founder APT Apostolic and Prophetic Women Network

This book is preventative and curative medicine for the destructive and distracting force called offenses. I recommend it to anyone who desires to be "offense-proof" in a world where offenses will surely come, as Jesus said. Mastering the principles shared will foster maturity and help the reader be at peace with all men.

Ruth N Bokwe, Class of Pluckys 77, Saker Baptist College Limbe Cameroon, Retired Public Administrator, Current CEO of Christy's Compassionate Care, Maryland, USA

Whether you are a mature Christian, or you are a newly saved Christian; reading this book will help you grow in your relationship with God, in your service and witness to others, and in your participation in the life of your local Church. It is practical and filled with biblical wisdom. With personal struggles, I found myself relating to some aspects in nearly every chapter. For me, taking offense with God amd man started with my disappointments in two relationships and losing my only daughter. It continued through years of depression that seemed to permit others to dismiss how I was vocalizing my feelings. I felt unworthy of respect from man and of love from both man and God. This book, *How to Handle Offenses*, reminds us all that God loves and shows us grace, and God's standard is, "to forgive others, as He has forgiven us of our sins." I am so proud that my sister in Christ, Dr Mercy Forlu, has distilled the wisdom of her many years of church leadership and marriage into this book on how to handle offenses in our daily living; for they are bound to happen.

Carmela Myles, Author Living in the Creative Realm, CarmelaMyles.com

In an era where the slightest misunderstanding can lead to deep divisions, Dr. Forlu offers a compelling and spiritually enriching exploration of offense through the lens of Scripture. Her insightful analysis begins with a foundational understanding of what constitutes an offense, delving into its root causes and the complex interplay of human emotions that lead individuals to offend and take offense. Drawing from the timeless wisdom of the Bible, Dr. Forlu examines the profound spiritual impact of offense. She provides a compassionate look at those who are easily offended, uncovering the layers of hurt and vulnerability that often lie beneath. Her work aligns with the teachings of Christ, who calls us to love, forgive, and seek reconciliation. Her approach underscores the weight and power of offense, urging readers to reflect on their own hearts and seek God's guidance in overcoming these challenges. Dr. Forlu offers a path towards healing and unity, making her work an essential read for anyone striving to live out their faith with compassion and grace.

Sister Ruth Collins. USA

I met sister Mercy in 1984 during a women's ministries conference in Cameroon, West Africa. I have known her to be a godly anointed speaker. This book aptly explains how to forgive and receive peace from God. I highly recommend that as you read this book, you put these principles into practice and enjoy the freedom of forgiveness and the gift of peace that comes to you from God. Thank you, Sister Mercy, for teaching and offering this much needed teaching. May God use this book to help many who have been offended and unable to find true peace through forgiveness.

HOW TO HANDLE OFFENSES

HOW TO HANDLE OFFENSES

Grace to Manifest the Power of Forgiveness

Mercy Forlu, Ph.D.

Purpose House Publishing

Published by PurposeHouse Publishing, Columbia, Maryland. Cover Design by PurposeHouse Publishing.

Printed in the USA.

ISBN: 978-1-957190-14-3

CONTENTS

FOREWORD

Dr. Elton Wayne Duke
Academic Advisor, Newburgh Theological Seminary and School of
the Bible

Most of my life has been devoted to pastoring, education, and training. I retired from Post-Secondary Education as a professor, instructor, and director. I currently pastor a church in western KY and serve as an Academic Advisor at Newburgh Theological Seminary and School of the Bible.

Through my thirty-plus years as an educator working with mainly 16-24-year-old students, I saw my share of those being offended and those who did the offense. In most cases, there was no reason for that person to be offended.

We live in a nation that is widely divided over many issues; many are offending and being offended. The problems that we have in this nation are not going to be resolved by our elected officials in Washington. We appear to be at a point of no compromise; it is my way or no way. The problems of offenses can only be resolved by divine intervention, but first, we must seek God.

I have had the pleasure of working with Dr. Mercy Forlu over the last few years as an Academic Advisor. I got to see first-hand her mission of love and care for others. Dr. Mercy Forlu has devoted her life to her husband, her children, her grandchildren, her work, her ministries, and most importantly to God.

This book, *How to Handle Offenses: Grace to Manifest the Power of Forgiveness*, is a diamond in the rough, a treasure that promises answers to many questions. I have read many books and reviewed many papers put together by students; I can promise you will be blessed by reading this book. You will see Dr. Mercy Forlu crafted her writing around nineteen chapters that go into detail on offenses. Her writing is not just her words, but backed by scripture, God's Word.

Read this book for knowledge. Read this book for Spiritual growth. Read this book to better understand both those who are offended and those who offend. Most importantly, read this book to find out God's solution to offenses.

ACKNOWLEDGEMENTS

I am deeply grateful to the Holy Spirit for His guidance and empowering presence, which has been essential in teaching me about forgiveness and handling offenses. Your insights, which align with Biblical teachings, have been invaluable.

Thank you, Sister Ruth Collins, for your pivotal role as a missionary in Cameroon. Your sermon on forgiveness and the idea of asking the Holy Spirit to plant the seed of forgiveness in one's heart greatly inspired me to write this book.

I appreciate my wonderful husband, friend, big brother, and Bishop, Dr. Israel Forlu, for your advice, financial support, prayers, and encouragement. Your unwavering support for everything God calls me to do means the world to me. I love you, Azeh (My Own), and thank you.

I am deeply grateful to my children—Gaius & Emmanuella Forlu, Jeremiah Benson and Nadege Forlu, Ryan and Danyel Forlu, Grace Forlu, and David and Bethany Forlu. Your loving care, prayers, and support have been instrumental in completing this book. Thank you for being a cherished blessing and joy to many generations.

I am profoundly grateful to my grandchildren—Lemuel Nyangaweh Forlu, Elianna Njweng Forlu, Jahzara Asoh Forlu, Samuel Nyangaweh Forlu, Daniel Lee-Alemnkia Forlu, Mercy Ann Forlu, Grace Lynn Forlu, Eliam Mercy Forlu, Hadassah Chayil Forlu, and Zendaya Njweng Forlu. Your calls, visits, and uplifting words and smiles have been a source of encouragement throughout my journey in writing this book. You are a cherished blessing and a joy to many generations.

I appreciate my River of Life Assemblies Int'l (ROLAI) family, especially The Women for Jesus and The Teens for Jesus, for your inspiration and encouragement.

I appreciate my classmates from Saker Baptist College Limbe Cameroon, fondly known as "The Pluckys" (Plucky 77). Your ongoing friendship and encouragement have been invaluable. Special thanks to Dr. Belinda Assam for fostering our lasting connection.

A heartfelt thanks to the pastors' wives of Pastors' Wives Arise Network International (PWANI). Your support and encouragement during our forums and conferences have been deeply appreciated.

I am also grateful to those who have offended me or may do so in the future. Your actions have brought me closer to God and deepened my understanding of forgiveness. I have come to realize that all things work for my good and God's glory.

To those whom I have offended and who have forgiven me, your grace has taught me valuable lessons reflected in this book. I am very grateful.

Thank you, Rev. Lenita Reeves, CEO of Purpose House Publishing, and your team, for your support and for being part of this journey. Your role as a publisher has been a great encouragement.

I acknowledge and appreciate my niece, Prisca Tangi, who is like a sister to me, for your unwavering support. Your prayers have been a true blessing. Thank you.

My sincere thanks to Newburgh Theological Seminary in Indiana. The education I received, including my B.A., M.A., and Ph.D., has been crucial in writing this book. I am especially grateful to all my professors, and particularly to Dr. Elton Wayne Duke, for taking the time to write the foreword. God bless you, Sir.

Finally, I express my gratitude to Bishop Dr. Israel Forlu, Dr. Julius Esunge, Dr. Kenneth Tah, Rev. Gaius Forlu, Dr. Francis Myles, Pastor Carmela Myles, Ms. Ruth Bokwe, Mrs. Ruth Collins, and Rev. Lenita Reeves for reviewing excerpts and endorsing my book. Your support means a great deal to me. Thank you all.

INTRODUCTION

OFFENSES MUST COME

Causing offense and taking offense are two things happening daily in this world. One person is causing offense, and another is taking offense. And sometimes, people take offense without a cause. In this book, I address how to deal with offenses in relationships (interpersonal relationships) with family, friends, work teams, and more. Moreover, I look especially at how God wants offenses solved in a local church family to restore broken relationships through the biblically prescribed reconciliatory method. And I write to help us understand that offenses can be intentional or unintentional. Jesus said, *"Woe to the world because of offenses! For offenses must come, but woe to that man by whom the offense comes!" (Matthew 18:7 NKJV).*

Offense is, therefore, inevitable. Offense is the key reason for broken relationships. Offense comes to everyone, Christian and non-Christian. Jesus said specifically about Christians, *"At that time many will be offended and repelled (by their association with Me) and will fall away (from the One whom they should trust) and will betray one another (handing over believers to their persecutors) and will hate one another" (Matthew 24:10 AMP).* In these last days, some Christians will break their relationship with Jesus and with one another because they will choose to take offense.

However, God wants us to be like Paul, who said, *"This being so, I myself always strive to have a conscience without offense toward God and men" (Acts 24:16 NKJV).* God's standard remains sure; forgiveness is what He expects from us, no matter the offense. His Word says in *Matthew 6:15, "But if you don't forgive others, then your Father in Heaven will not forgive the wrongs you do" (ERV).*

There are different types of offenses. However, as mentioned earlier, I am focusing on offenses affecting interpersonal relationships, such as marriages, friends, family, church family, and colleagues in a work team. When two or more people come together to live in one house or work in an establishment, there are bound to

be offenses. This is because we do not all reason or feel the same. As

our faces are different, so are our minds, temperaments, beliefs,

values, and more. According to Cloud and Townsend, "Wherever

two are gathered, there will be conflict.

But this is not bad. Conflict just means that two things come

together that are opposed to each other and do not immediately

agree."[1] What will be good in any conflict is that the people

concerned work through it and understand each other without

causing or taking offense. It has not always been so; great offenses

have resulted from little conflicts.

Nevertheless, offenses allow us to practice forgiveness. With

the understanding that offenses must surely happen as long as we are

in this world, we can decide to purpose in our hearts to value our

relationships (especially the ones we know are God-given),

---

[1] Dr. Henry Cloud and Dr. John Townsend, *Boundaries in Marriage* (Grand Rapids, MI: Zondervan, 1999), 197.

anticipate offense, and determine to dialogue and resolve the issues with a ready heart to forgive.

We must forgive so that God will also forgive us. Love and forgiveness are key ingredients in building healthy, peaceful relationships and restoring broken ones.

CHAPTER 1

WHAT IS AN OFFENSE?

An offense can be defined as a violation of the law, custom, or rule. According to the law, an offense is any illegal act, public wrong, or crime. Simply said, an offense is wrongdoing. Every wrong action, thought, or word is an offense, first against God and then against man. An offense is an action or words that cause a person to feel hurt, humiliated, angry, or displeased. Offenses can trigger negative emotional responses from the offended.

There are many different types of offenses, such as personal, sexual, violation offenses, and more. For example, if someone is driving a car and runs a red light, that is an offense against the law. And there are repercussions set in place when those offenses are committed. But that is not the type of offense I write about in this book.

As mentioned, I am focusing on offenses affecting interpersonal relationships. Many times, these types of offenses may not be against our legal laws, so the authorities may not do anything when they happen, but they are still very real in the hearts and minds of the offended. For example, a certain lady took offense because she heard someone make sly comments about her daughter. She could not take the matter to the police, but the offense was alive and real in her heart. That is the type of offense I am talking about.

If you guard your heart, you will not easily take offense. You will be slow to anger, as God's Word says, which is good for you because some people struggle so long to let go when offended.

Offense is a big weapon that the devil uses to lead many people astray, especially Christians. The devil uses offense as bait to get believers to be trapped in unforgiveness and displease God. He deceives people into believing it is okay to stay angry and bitter against an offender until they apologize. He lies to you that you can be angry and resent people and that it is okay because, after all, you are just giving them what they deserve for the wrong they did to you.

But by so doing, you are offending God and endangering your life. God's way is for you to settle matters with your offenders and live in peace.

Jesus said you should take heed that no one deceives you. The devil can deceive you; people can deceive you, and you can also deceive yourself. So, take heed that no one deceives you.

The devil uses offense as bait to get believers to be trapped in unforgiveness and displease God. He deceives people into believing it is okay to stay angry and bitter against an offender until they apologize.

If someone did something wrong to you and comes around you or you think about them and you immediately feel hurt in your heart or emotionally disturbed, the reason might be you have taken offense against them. Everyone needs the grace of God not to easily take offense and to not be the person who causes offenses. As the Scriptures say, offenses must come, but woe to that person by whom the offense comes. It implies that it will not go well with the offender.

There is already a "woe" labeled on the one who causes an offense (Matthew 18:7), so you who are offended should have no business trying to retaliate. Instead, take care of your heart first, in the light of God's Word. Then, do your best to seek peace and reconciliation, so the offense does not destroy you.

Reflection

1. There are different types of offenses, and those that do not violate laws can still cause deep inner wounds. What types of offenses have you endured, and how did they affect your emotions? What, if any, negative emotions were triggered?

2. Offenses are like bait because the devil uses them to lure Christians into believing they don't need to forgive. Are there any offenses you have not dealt with and need God's grace to forgive?

CHAPTER 2

CAUSES OF OFFENSE

Wrong words cause offense.

There are many causes of offense; however, most offenses are caused by wrong words, actions, or attitudes. The Bible says in *Proverbs 25:11, "A word fitly spoken is like apples of gold in settings of silver" (NJKV).* Proverbs 15:1 says, *"A soft answer turns away wrath, but a harsh word stirs up anger."* Whether in conversation, dialogues, or giving responses to your spouse, friend, sibling, co-worker, or church member, the right words fitly spoken will ensure peace, good understanding, and harmony in every relationship. The Bible also says in *Proverbs 18:21, "Death and life are in the power of the tongue, and those who love it will eat its fruits."* With the tongue, people bless others, and with the tongue, people hurt others.

The tongue can cause war; it can also cause peace. To live peaceably with people, you must speak kind and good words that do not offend. Be it at home with your spouse and children, at work with colleagues, or interacting with members of a church family, yelling or shouting at someone, cursing, talking rudely, gossiping, speaking lies, making false accusations and false witness, and slandering can cause offense, and destroy relationships.

The tongue can cause war; it can also cause peace.

Words carry much impact. Words, whether written or spoken, affect our spouses, children, classmates, work colleagues, business associates, neighbors, brethren at church, and friends, positively or negatively. No wonder the Bible says we will have to give an account of every idle word we speak. *"But I say to you that for every idle word men may speak, they will give account of it in the day of judgement" (Matthew 12:36 NKJV).* The tongue is like dynamite, which influences our relationship with God, our relationship with the people we treasure the most, and even ourselves.

Wrong actions and attitudes cause offense.

There is an inexhaustible list of wrong actions people manifest that can be offensive. Such as, but not limited to:

- Hatred

- Stealing

- Cheating

- Murder

- Rape

- Rejection

- Neglect

- Abuse

- Despite

- Assault

- Jealousy and more

Many relationships have been broken because of offenses from wrong actions. Many are feeling hurt because of offenses.

One of the causes of offense I wish to address is that which occurs when a married person refuses sexual intimacy with their spouse. After our relationship with God, the husband and wife relationship is a vital relationship on Earth. Lack of sexual intimacy in marriage can result in unnecessary problems, which can end up in divorce. God created sex for the pleasure of married couples, and the joy of it satisfies the couple and strengthens their bond.

God designed sex and meant it to be enjoyed and fulfilling for both husband and wife. So, if you're not connected sexually, that's not a healthy marriage. Next to your relationship with God, your marriage takes precedence, and meeting one another's needs is vital. When a husband and wife are connected spiritually, physically, and emotionally, you have a marriage that can stand the test of time. With God as the center and both individuals surrendered to Him, you can overcome anything.[2]

This is so true. I am married to my one and only husband of forty-three years and counting. I understand the joy, satisfaction, and true bonding from our sexual intimacy. And the joy and happiness that my husband always expresses is very pronounced. Any marriage that does not enjoy sexual success is bound to have problems and challenges that can lead to offenses and a broken relationship. The married couple could agree to abstain for some time for righteous reasons but come back together again to avoid temptations. *1 Corinthians 7:5 says, "Don't refuse to give your bodies to each other. But you might both agree to stay away from sex for a while so that you can give your time to prayer. Then come together again so that Satan will not be able to tempt you in your weakness" (ERV).* The offense of infidelity and more could happen when couples are not having successful sexual intimacy. Douglas Weiss says:

---

[2] Joni Lamb, *Surrender All: Your Answer to Living with Peace, Power, and Purpose* (Colorado Springs, CO: Warterbrook & Multnomah, 2008), 59-60.

The ability to connect with your spouse in three God-given dimensions–spirit, soul, and body – can satisfy you so profoundly that you do not even desire sex the next day. Imagine being that sexually satiated on a regular basis; that is sexual success![3]

Rejection as One Cause of Offense

People may reject others due to personal incompatibility, fear or insecurity, past experiences, social norms, lack of empathy, miscommunication, or personal issues. When parents are unable to adequately care for their children, possibly due to their own personal challenges, it can lead to feelings of neglect and hurt in the kids. Some children may experience a sense of rejection, feeling uncherished and believing that they are not cared for. As a result, they may seek acceptance and love from inappropriate sources, which can lead to destructive behavior and strained relationships

---

[3] Douglas Weiss, *Sex, Men and God: A Godly Man's Road Map to Sexual Success* (Lake Mary, FL: Siloam/Strang, 2002), 1.

with their parents.

Rejection inflicts deep emotional pain in spouses, friends, children, and others. It has become a significant trigger for offenses that demand attention today. Many individuals who experience rejection often spiral into depression and, in severe cases, contemplate suicide. Addressing feelings of rejection and fostering acceptance and support are crucial for preventing such harmful outcomes. Dr. Elizabeth Fondong says this about rejection:

> The spirit of rejection is an oppressive spirit that causes people to feel unwanted, unloved, and not useful. It usually comes from abandonment and childhood trauma, but it can also come through betrayal, losses, and disappointments in adulthood. The spirit of rejection comes in through a lie that a person believes. It can also cause ungodly attachments and entanglements that make no room for attachments to God. This is the beginning of idolatry. The spirit of rejection

makes you feel there is no body to help.[4]

Rejection in marriage can have significant emotional and psychological consequences, leading to feelings of loneliness, resentment, and, ultimately, marital breakdown if not addressed and resolved through open communication and mutual respect.

Causing offense can be intentional or unintentional.

Causing Offense Intentionally

This is when an offense is done knowingly, which means it was a deliberate act, pre-planned, consciously calculated or determined, or done on purpose. Crystabelle Ferim's statement is true:

> As much as demonic forces can project this, there is also wickedness in the thoughts and hearts of men that could be detrimental to another man. *Genesis 6:5 states: 'And God saw that the wickedness of man was great in the earth, and*

---

[4] Dr. Elizabeth Fondong, *Freedom from the Spirit of Rejection: Receiving the Father's Love, Rejecting the Enemy's Lies* (Amazon Digital Services LLC, 2021), 79.

that every imagination of the thoughts of his heart was only evil continually.' (KJV). Wickedness can, therefore, be acted upon, an intent of the heart, or thought out. Many people sit and craft crazy things that could inflict much pain on others.[5]

Yes, it is so true that bad people devise evil against others. And because man's heart is not exposed to other people, except by some divine revelation, it is hard to tell what anyone is planning in their hearts. Offense can, therefore, be intentional, and this is happening every day in the world through people inspired by the devil.

Causing Offense Unintentionally

This is when an offense is done unknowingly, which means the act was accidental, not planned, or the offender was unaware that they were causing an offense. Some actions or reactions could stem from one's perspective or perception. Sometimes, someone's

---

[5] Crystabelle Ferim, *The Solitary Journey of the Called* (Dallas, TX: Primedia eLaunch LLC, 2022), 84.

upbringing, which involves their core values, could influence them to say or do things a certain way without the slightest thought that they are offending someone. Some of these actions cause easily resolvable conflicts, while some result in long-term conflicts involving offenses and bitterness.

Reflection

1. Wrong words, actions, and attitudes can cause offenses, and people can unintentionally or intentionally cause offenses.

    a. Have any of the wrong actions listed in this chapter caused offenses in your life?

    b. Have you considered whether they were deliberately or unintentionally perpetrated, and how does this influence your ability to forgive?

2. Have you ever unintentionally offended someone? If so, how did the other party's perception influence the offense? Did you seek forgiveness? If so, how was the matter resolved?

3. If married, have you ever intentionally withheld sex from

your spouse because of an offense? What were the

consequences and effects on your relationship?

CHAPTER 3

WHO DO PEOPLE OFFEND?

People cause offenses against individuals, families, communities, etc. And, of course, all real offenses (sins) are against God because God is Holy, and He is the only one who cannot offend in any way. God is not pleased when we offend one another because He wants us to follow peace with all men and holiness, without which no man shall see Him (Hebrews 12:14). We offend God daily in our thoughts, words, and deeds, yet He shows us mercy whenever we ask Him. But He will judge anyone who refuses to acknowledge their wrongs and repent. Jim Lynn comments on man and offenses:

> God has a legal problem with man. Every human being old enough to know right from wrong has committed offenses against God, a crime which carries with it capital punishment

(1 Corinthians 15:56). The law we violate, though good, is one no man can keep. It is called the law of sin and death (Ezekiel 18:4; Romans 8:1-2). And though we are not able to keep this law (Romans 3:23), we are without excuse and stand convicted. For God has made Himself known to us (Romans 1:20; 3:10). His judgement of guilt is just (Romans 3: 19-20).[6]

We all offend God with our sins, yet God has provided a way out of sin for us through the death of His Son, Jesus Christ, on the cross. He is willing to forgive us if we accept the gift of His Son in our lives and allow Him to transform us.

Individuals in a relationship experience offense; one offends the other, and vice versa. In some relationships, one person is always prone to causing offenses and making the relationship suffer. So many relationships are broken because of offenses. In some families,

---

[6] Jim Lynn, *The Miracle of Healing in Your Church Today: Good health is not a matter of chance; it is your birthright* (Trafford Publishing, 2007), 124.

you may have one person who always puts the family members at loggerheads, always causing misunderstandings and throwing words of confusion that can separate the family members.

> *Individuals in a relationship experience offense; one offends the other, and vice versa. So many relationships are broken because of offenses.*

A local church is considered a family and a community. Sometimes, when a church or community member sins against God, for example, stealing or committing immorality, it is considered an offense against the local church or community, even though it is a sin against God. That offense impacts the local church family, community, county, or state. Some members may take offense. They may grumble, murmur, complain, blame, and disassociate themselves from that local church or community because of the offense.

An individual can offend himself by saying bad words, cursing himself, or doing foolish actions against his own body and regrets or gets hurt.

Reflection

1. How should knowing God forgives us when we offend Him daily affect how we handle being offended by others?

2. People can offend others, God, communities, families, and themselves. One community that is often offended is the local church. Have any offenses affected your relationships with church members, the pastor, or church attendance? If so, how?

CHAPTER 4

TAKING OFFENSE

Taking offense can manifest in various ways and forms, such as:

- Annoyance

- Indignation

- Anger

- Protest

- Feeling humiliated

- Acts or words of retaliation

- Displeasure

- Resentment

- Grudges

- Bitterness and more

Taking offense manifests inwardly and outwardly. Inwardly as an annoyance, ill-feeling, humiliation, hurt, displeasure, indignation, anger, agitation, or bitterness. It manifests outwardly as protest, acts of retaliation, physical fighting, murder, cursing, and more.

Two Ways of Taking Offense

Taking offense is in two categories:

1. Wrongfully taking offense

2. Rightfully taking offense

Wrongfully Taking Offense

Taking offense wrongfully means you were not supposed to be offended but chose to be. To wrongfully take offense means that whatever happened had no substance of offense, but the offended person claimed offense.

Sometimes, this happens when:

a. Someone is reproved, rebuked, or corrected, even in the most

appropriate way:

2 Timothy 4:2 says, *"Preach the word! Be ready in season and*

out of season. Convince, rebuke, exhort, with all longsuffering

and teaching" (NKJV). Luke 17:3 says, "Take heed to

yourselves. If your brother sins against you, rebuke him; and

if he repents, forgive him. " Some people don't like to be

corrected. Some Christians get angry when they hear God's

Word, which comes to them as a rebuke. Some get angry with

the preacher and start complaining. They may start gossiping

about the preacher, slandering him from one person to another.

In a local church where I used to attend, a man and his wife

attended church together. The pastor preached a good message

about sin, repentance, and God's forgiveness. After the church

service, the husband was angry and offended with his wife. He

accused her of going behind his back and revealing things

about him to the pastor. The wife sincerely told him that was not the case, and I do not remember how the matter was resolved.

b. There's a misunderstanding amongst brethren or acquaintances:

From a little misunderstanding, someone could wrongfully take offense over something with which another person may find no problem. Any inadequate or wrong communication can result in misunderstanding because the listener is placed in a position to assume or imagine things wrongly since they do not see the whole picture of whatever is being communicated to them.

c. There is wrong or poor judgment:

Not everyone has good judgement. People judge things based on their perspective, core values, cultural upbringing, and understanding of the subject. And so, someone may be wrongfully taking offense concerning a matter without knowing they are wrong. Maybe with time or a change of location, they realize their folly and learn from their mistakes.

In my home country, Cameroon, a young lady who lived in a particular community went to work wearing pants. In that community, especially in her church in those days, it was forbidden for ladies to wear pants because it was believed that pants were meant only for men (men's attire). And so, her church considered it a sin for ladies to put on pants. This lady worked with an electricity company, and on this day, she had to join the team that had to go up an electric pole to do some repairs. She decided to wear pants because she felt that wearing a dress or skirt would expose her underwear while she was up the ladder. Some brethren who saw her on her way to work were very offended, and it became the talk of the church. Imagine how many brethren had gossiped about her and called her unfaithful to God and a backslider. She had to explain herself only after she, too, had been offended by hurtful words against her. The matter was resolved, but some of those with wrong judgement later traveled out of the country and realized that the world was not limited to their community, and today, many of them who considered the wearing of pants by ladies to be a sin, are now putting on pants during snow, to protect themselves from the cold of the snow. Their judgement changed with the process of time, the change of location, and a better understanding of the Scriptures. They have dropped their wrong beliefs and learned to embrace people correctly.

d. Someone is offended by the truth, the Gospel, or God's children (just because they are God's children):
When I newly gave my life to Christ, some of my relations were offended that my life was changed for good. Some friends were also offended because I could not cooperate with the wrong things we used to do together. They wrongfully took offense.

e. There is jealousy:
Some people get jealous, feeling that the good that happened to their friend should have happened to them. Others get offended just by seeing another person make progress in life.

f. There is hunger:

Some people take offense and get angry when they are

hungry, especially when they do not consider that the

circumstances that kept them hungry were reasonable. They

wrongfully take offense. This can happen with husbands who

are not reasonable towards their wives. I remember before my

father gave his life to Christ, he used to be so offended and

beat my mother when he was hungry if his food was served

late. Thank God he changed when he gave his life to Christ.

g. There is sickness:

Some people take offense and even blame God and others for

their sicknesses, even when the people they blame are not

responsible. By so doing, they could mar their relationship

with God and man. And, of course, God should never be

blamed for anything evil or bad.

h. There is misinterpretation:

Some people wrongfully take offense when they misinterpret

actions and words. Many quarrels and troubles that brought

separation happened in families, churches, and even larger communities because people wrongfully took offense when misinterpreting the words or actions of others.

i.   Expectations are not met:

For example, John the Baptist. *Matthew 11:2-6 says, "Now when John had heard in the prison the works of Christ, he sent two of his disciples, and said unto him, Art thou he that should come, or do we look for another? Jesus answered and said unto them, Go and shew John again those things which ye do hear and see: The blind receive their sight, and the lame walk, the lepers are cleansed, and the deaf hear, the dead are raised up, and the poor have the gospel preached to them. And blessed is he, whosoever shall not be offended in me" (KJV).* John was in prison because of the Gospel, and he expected Jesus to visit him, but that did not happen. Because of this, he became offended with Jesus and even started doubting if Jesus was the promised Messiah. Interestingly, John proudly proclaimed Jesus to the people when he was not in prison.

"The next day John seeth Jesus coming unto him, and saith, "behold the Lamb of God, which taketh away the sin of the world" (John 1:29 KJV). But when he was offended, he began to doubt Jesus and even asked if Jesus was the Messiah. Even today, some Christians take offense, either at God or man, when their expectations are not met. People in courtship, married couples, children and parents, and friends could get offended with one another when their expectations are not met.

j.   People just decide to be the opposition:

The Pharisees and the Sadducees also took offense against Jesus for saying that He was the Son of God. When Jesus spoke about what defiles a man, they were also offended. Jesus said in *Matthew 15:11-12, "Not what goes into the mouth defiles a man; but what comes out of the mouth, this defiles a man." Then His disciples came and said to Him, 'Do you know that the Pharisees were offended when they heard this saying?"* When Jesus said, "Before Abraham was, I AM," the Pharisees were offended (John 8:58). They wrongfully took offense against Jesus.

In the same way, lack of knowledge and understanding can cause people to take offense against God and one another. The Pharisees and Sadducees did not get the light. They were religious leaders who seemed to have thought that Jesus came to challenge them with a new religion contrary to what they had always known. They were always trying to prove a point against Jesus, so they were the set of people who just decided to be the opposition group against Jesus.

No one ought to take offense against God. Jesus said, *"Blessed is he, whosoever shall not be offended in me" (Matthew 11:6 KJV).*

The person who is offended is vulnerable to the devil's attacks. Choose not to be offended. Run to God for help. Taking offense can be a choice. If one is filled with the Holy Spirit, has good knowledge and understanding of God's Word, and manifests the fruit of the Holy Spirit, it will be difficult for such a person to wrongfully take offense.

Taking offense is in two categories: wrongfully and rightfully taking offense. Taking offense wrongfully means you were not supposed to be offended but chose to be.

Rightfully Taking Offense

To rightfully take offense means that you have every right to be offended. You have every right to be mad or angry because the person truly wronged you through no fault of your own. In such circumstances, even God will agree that you have the right to be angry.

But even though you are angry, God doesn't want you to sin in your anger. *"Be angry, and sin not: let not the sun go down upon your wrath" (Ephesians 4:26 KJV).* Sinning in your anger means saying the wrong things, having the wrong thoughts, or acting in the wrong ways. And if you rightfully take offense, by sunset, the Lord expects you to forgive and let go of the anger. Jesus was angry but did not sin, so we must be like Him.

God cannot ask of you what you cannot do. He has given you the Holy Spirit to help you, and you must rely on Him to help you. You must remain pure in your heart when you are angry. Your thoughts should reflect what *Philippians 4:8* says, *"Finally, brethren, whatsoever things are true, whatsoever things are honest, whatsoever things are just, whatsoever things are pure, whatsoever things are lovely, whatsoever things are of good report, if there be any virtue, and if there be any praise, think on these things" (KJV). Ecclesiastes 7:9 says, "Don't become too angry quickly, because anger is foolish" (ERV)*. God expects us to be slow to anger. *Proverbs 16:32 says, "He who is slow to anger is better than the mighty, and he who rules his spirit than he who takes a city" (NKJV)*. The Holy Spirit can help us to be slow to anger.

If you rightfully take offense, it means that whatever wrong happened, your taking of offense is justified by God and man. Jesus rightfully took offense and did what was right, as seen in *John 2:15-16, which says, "Jesus made a whip with some pieces of rope. Then he forced all these men and the sheep and cattle to leave the Temple*

area. He turned over the tables of the money traders and scattered

their money. Then He said to those who were selling pigeons, 'take

these things out of here! Don't make my Father's house a place for

buying and selling!" (ERV). Jesus drove the traders out of God's

house with anger, with a whip, to give them an understanding of how

grievous their actions were. It's like a father correcting a child with a

whip, with a heart full of love towards the child. He did that with

authority and love, not as an enemy. From that time, we have no

more Biblical record of people selling and buying in God's house.

Jesus corrected the situation with strictness and firmness.

Also, God can get angry with you for not forgiving your

fellow man, and He can allow certain bad things to happen to you to

call you to order. *"And his lord was wroth, and delivered him to the*

tormentors, till he should pay all that was due unto him. So likewise

shall my heavenly Father do also unto you, if ye from your hearts

forgive not everyone his brother their trespasses" (Matthew 18:34-

35 KJV). Dennis Lim comments on an aspect of God's anger:

Anger can be constructive if it leads us to help the person who hurt us or another. Christ angrily told Peter to "get behind me" (Mt. 16:23) because He loved Peter and wanted him to grow by facing the approaching "suffering in Jerusalem." (Mt. 18:34), Christ's anger blazes forth. Christ doesn't just silently withdraw, swallow his anger and hope injustice will disappear. Anger drives him to correct injustices quickly even before night falls.[7]

Reflection

1. The chapter lists several ways we can wrongfully take offense. Which of the listed ways have you experienced, and how can you handle such situations in the future?

2. We can rightfully or wrongfully take offense. How does Jesus' example show us how to handle rightfully being offended?

---

[7] Dennis Linn & Matthew Linn, *Healing Life's Hurts: Healing Memories through Five Stages of Forgiveness* (New York, NY: Paulist Press, 1978), 105.

CHAPTER 5

PEOPLE TAKE OFFENSE AGAINST WHO?

People Take Offense Against God

Some people get offended with God because He didn't do something for them or permitted something bad to happen to them or someone they care about. Some get mad at God for the things happening in the world or how world rulers run their various governments. Anger towards God normally manifests in scenarios that are beyond our control.

When you feel helpless and feel God is not acting as He should, you may be tempted to take offense. In her book *Door of Hope*, Jan Frank wrote that she was in a women's retreat, sharing her "Free to Care" recovery steps for healing emotional wounds when she noticed a lady called Joanne (who initially appeared trouble-free and related well with other women). Joanne was weeping in the arms of a friend.

> Several minutes after speaking, I was able to work my way
> back to Joanne. I reached out and put my arms around her as
> she choked out these words, 'I've never let myself cry since I
> lost my little boy six years ago. He was only ten months old
> when he died. After all these years, I'm still angry at God.'
> Joanne gazed into my eyes and said, when you spoke tonight,
> Jan, I had never fully faced Timmy's death. I've never let
> myself grieve completely.[8]

Joanne was offended with God because her son died. She
probably thought God did that to hurt her, but that was not the case.
God doesn't offend us. Job is reported in the Bible as one who lost
all his children in one day, yet he did not take offense against God.
God is altogether good, and He does only good to us. Though He
may sometimes allow trouble to happen to us, He always makes
things work out for our good. *"And we know that all things work*

---

[8] Jan Frank, *Door of Hope: Recognizing and Resolving the Pains of Your Past* (Nashville, TN: Thomas Nelson, 1995), 1.

together for good to those who love God, to those who are the called according to His purpose" (Romans 8:28 NKJV).

People take offense against people.

It could be something someone has done to hurt you, or you may be angry at a group (society, government, etc.) for an injustice you believe they committed against you or a loved one. When conflicts occur, people may or may not take offense, depending on their level of understanding, their stance, and the disposition of their hearts. In any relationship, wrong or inadequate communication may lead to misunderstanding, misinterpretation, and, consequently, offense. The inability to accommodate each other's differences could also occur because of differences in core values, perspectives, perceptions, or even expectations concerning roles. Bad behaviors such as sinful and self-seeking desires, defensiveness, and being scornful easily bring offenses in relationships. Sometimes, a person may behave or speak a certain way because of low self-esteem, offending others.

When people have personality clashes, offenses are also

inevitable. If you live with someone who is always blaming and seeing faults in almost everything, offenses are inevitable. Relationships such as friends, siblings, married couples, and others have always experienced conflicts and offenses. It seems people cannot dwell together without friction, conflicts, or offense.

However, some conflicts are constructive, especially if the people concerned focus on resolving the problem rather than on the personality defects of one another. When both parties truly love and care for each other and are determined to keep their relationship, they will focus on the problem as they confront each other or when they meet a counselor to solve the matter. They will not seek to destroy one another. Dr. Tembi says this of constructive conflict:

> Conflict is a fact of life. In any on-going relationship, whether at home, at church or ministry, at the jobsite or social groups, anywhere people come together, it is inevitable. Conflicts can be healthy and constructive if the parties give adequate attention to handling it well. Constructive conflicts will bring important issues out in the

open, resulting in lasting solutions to problems and closeness

between the parties after the conflict.[9]

Some conflicts are constructive, especially if the people concerned focus on resolving the problem rather than on the personality defects of one another.

People get offended with themselves.

You can be angry at yourself for countless reasons. It could

be based on your actions, bad choices, or things you did or didn't do

that, in turn, greatly affected your life or those you care about. The

Word of God clearly tells us not to be unequally yoked with

unbelievers, and every child of God who wants to please God must

obey His Word. Some decisions people make end up creating a life

filled with offenses and regrets, especially a believer in Christ

getting married to an unbeliever. They are moving spiritually in

opposite directions because one person has their understanding

---

[9] Dr. Beatrice Tembi, *Help! I'm a Wife!: A Woman's Guide to Navigating the Married Life* (Richardson, TX: IEM Press. 2019), 34.

enlightened in the things of God, and the other hasn't. So, there are bound to be problems. Terry Hadaway speaks of this disharmony:

> Another problem in our families is spiritual disharmony. The Biblical instruction is clear–do not marry unbelievers (2 Corinthians 6:14). Like any other violation of Biblical principles, violation of this principle has consequences–unhappiness, mistrust, unfaithfulness, and divorce are all real consequences that people face every day. Some unbelieving spouses eventually do come to faith in God, but the years leading up to that decision can leave permanent scars on the relationship.[10]

Many have caused a lot of pain for themselves by running into great problems through wrong choices and the pursuit of things to satisfy their desires or fulfill their needs in life, after which they get offended with themselves, become full of regrets, and even

---

[10] Billy Graham Literary Trust and Terry Hadaway, *Building a Christ-Centered Home* (Nashiville,TN: Thomas Nelson, 2007), 74.

become suicidal. If you do not want to offend yourself and others, you must obey God's Word, trusting the Holy Spirit to help you. Lawrence Crabb describes the consequences of searching for significance outside of Christ:

> Because people are both physical beings and personal beings, they have both physical needs and personal needs. Physical needs consist of whatever is needed to physically survive, to keep the body alive—food, clothing, shelter, etc. Personal needs consist of whatever is required to personally survive, to keep the person alive—significance and security as a basis for self-worth . . . Many people are in the process of dying and do not realize their plight. As long as they entertain the hope that more money, fame, prestige, sex, travel, whatever will provide them with significance and security, they keep going. As soon as they face the horrid blackness of no worth and no hope of attaining it, a deep, overwhelming despair sets in. At that point, they either suicide, have a nervous breakdown, become psychotically withdrawn or bizarre, or

plunge into irrational efforts to dull the pain (alcohol, drugs, running away, pornography, etc.). When a person grasps the truth that he is significant and secure in Christ and begins to practice that truth by rational, responsible, obedient, and committed living, he becomes whole, alive, vibrant, and full.[11]

That is why you should pray before you make decisions. If you know that God is your Father, He loves you, knows it all, and is willing to help you, you must let Him lead you. If He does, you will save yourself from much pain. *"In all your ways acknowledge Him, And He shall direct your paths" (Proverbs 3:6 NKJV).*

Whether you are offended and angry with people, yourself, or God, you must find a way to let go of the offense and move on with your life—that way is Jesus Christ. You will have a better quality of life if you let go of anger and bitterness.

---

[11] Lawrence Crabb Jr., *Effective Biblical Counseling* (Grand Rapids, MI: Zondervan, 1977), 114.

Reflection

1. Being offended and angry with God usually results from scenarios beyond our control, for example, the loss of a loved one. Have you ever felt that God let you down and become offended? How does Romans 8:28 apply to such situations?

2. When and why are some conflicts constructive? How can you handle offense constructively?

3. Under what circumstances can people become offended with themselves, and how can that be avoided?

CHAPTER 6

TAKING OFFENSE IS A CHOICE

I believe that taking offense is a choice. Offense is like a place you can choose to reside or not. Offense is like an event that you can choose to attend or not. Offenses will come in many ways, but it's up to you to choose either to take offense or purpose in your heart not to take offense and move on with your life.

Because offenses may come daily in different ways, you need to brace up against them with the Word of God, which is the sword of the Spirit. For your peace of mind, it's good to live offense-free. It's also important to remember that each time you take offense, you put yourself on a battlefield, making yourself vulnerable to diabolic attacks and defeat.

You can intentionally purpose in your heart to lean on the Holy Spirit to help you choose not to take offense, just like Paul who said, *"And herein do I exercise myself, to have always a conscience void of offense toward God, and toward men" (Acts 24:16 KJV).* This means we can exercise ourselves to be void of offense. Specifically, we can do this by loving the Word of God, being students of the Word, feeding on it daily, and relying on the Holy Spirit to help us to obey it; being prayerful, practicing, and staying in that place of intimacy with the Lord Jesus; being quick to listen, slow to speak, and slow to get angry. These are all godly virtues that we can exercise, with the help of the Holy Spirit, keeping our consciences free of offense.

Your soul and mind are at peace when you choose not to take offense. You are physically and spiritually healthy with such a choice. On this earth, good people are offended, and bad people are offended. The Bible says offenses most surely come. The offenses do not come because you like them, but they come anyway. And when they come, they bring heartaches and pains.

How you choose to respond to bad circumstances can make or break you. Offense is trouble, and it can really be big trouble, depending on the stance of the offended. John W. Walton also explains that your choice of what you will say or do matters when it comes to moments like that:

> We will all have our share of heartache, but the way we respond makes all the difference in the world. Life is not always a celebration, but it is pleasing and satisfying if we can figure out how to confront our disappointments well. We can choose to shake off the setbacks and get on with it, or we can wallow in our troubles. It all comes down to choice, doesn't it?[12]

God allows offense to test your heart.

Sometimes, God will permit someone to offend you or a bad situation to occur so that you can see what's in your heart and know what is hidden inside of you that would never be revealed had that incident not happened. He will allow circumstances to test you,

---

[12] John W. Walton, *Compassionate Care: An Inspirational Guide For Caregivers Of The Seriously Ill*, (Maitland, FL: Xulon Press, 2007), 114.

show you what you need to fix about yourself, and help you understand how much you need Him and how much you must depend on Him.

How you choose to respond to bad circumstances can make or break you.

The Scriptures reveal a woman, in what I think was a difficult and challenging circumstance, who exercised faith in Jesus without taking offense.

Then Jesus went out from there and departed to the region of Tyre and Sidon. And behold, a woman of Canaan came from that region and cried out to Him, saying, 'Have mercy on me, O Lord, Son of David! My daughter is severely demon-possessed.' But He answered her not a word. And His disciples came and urged Him, saying, 'Send her away, for she cries out after us.' But He answered and said, 'I was not sent except to the lost sheep of the house of Israel.' Then she came and worshipped Him, saying, 'Lord help me!' But He answered and said, 'it is not good to take the children's bread and throw it to the little dogs.' And she said, 'Yes, Lord, yet even the little dogs eat the crumbs which fall from their masters' table.' Then Jesus answered and said to her, 'O woman, great is your faith! Let it be to you as you desire.' And her daughter was healed from that very hour. (Matthew 15:21-28 NKJV)

This passage shows that this woman had a big problem. She was in trouble because her daughter was possessed by a demon. She needed Jesus to deliver her daughter.

When she asked Jesus for help, He initially did not answer her a word. She persisted, and when He finally spoke, He said something like (putting it in my own words), "I did not come for you. I came but for the lost sheep of Israel; what you are asking for is not yours, and you have no right to it." Interesting! When He said, "It is not good to take the children's bread and throw it to the little dogs," I think it was a moment that could have caused this lady to become angry, but she was not.

Now, in moments like these, some people will throw a fit. They will get mad and offended that this "so-called Man of God" just insulted them simply because they asked for help. They probably would have insulted Jesus and riled up everyone to turn against Him. The possibilities are endless.

But that is not what this woman did. She chose not to be offended. Instead, when what seemed like an offense came, she chose to worship the Lord. She humbled herself before Him, accepted His words, and still spoke to Him with humility and respect. "Yes, Lord," she said, "Even the little dogs eat the crumbs that fall from their master's table."

God was pleased with her response. Her actions showed what was in her heart. She had a good and upright spirit, and because of that, she received her breakthrough exactly as she desired. Jesus answered, "O woman, great is your faith! Let it be to you as you desire." She got what she wanted. She was satisfied, and her joy was restored.

This woman is an example of someone who chose not to take offense, even when the situation presented itself as offensive. It is good to have a good understanding and the right disposition of heart in all things and circumstances. This comes with the help of the Holy Spirit.

In his book *Silent Struggler: A Caregiver's Personal Story*, Dr. Glenn Mollette wrote about his struggles while caring for his wife, Karen. Talk about an experience of "for better or for worse," as couples say on their wedding day. This was a "for worse" experience in his life. It was a very trying period—a period of heart testing. To my joy, as I read this book, this man was not bitter, and for the most part, he struggled silently, still loving God and his wife. There were moments when his wife verbally abused him, yet he still loved and cared for her as a loving, faithful, and dependable husband.

> While in the grip of depression, Karen would become verbally abusive. I didn't like this behavior, of course, but I understood what was happening to her . . . Making love to a person who has been verbally abusive and extremely critical

of everything you are trying to do for them isn't easy. It just isn't. but you must consider the other person.[13]

Being verbally abusive to a husband who is sacrificing all his life to be a sole caregiver to you is offensive. Yet, to the best of my understanding, Dr. Glenn Mollette persevered in love and took no offense against his wife. This is an example of a relationship well-guarded and kept in the period of "for worse"—the time of trouble. Indeed, he is an example of someone who chose not to be bitter with his sick wife. He notes the price of standing by her side.

I have seen Karen struggle and weep. I have struggled and wept with her. She has been in the depths of despair. I have been in the depths of despair with her. You can't love someone and care for them and stand idly by and watch them battle extreme physical and emotional pain without paying a toll. Sometimes, the price is tremendous.[14]

---

[13] Dr. Glenn Mollette, *Silent Struggler: A Caregiver's Personal Story* (Inspiration Press, 2000), 73.
[14] Ibid., 137.

I believe this statement came from his heart; it was based on the disposition of his heart.

Some other people would take offense and abandon their spouse to relatives and go their way. Some couples are divorced today because the worst situation came, and one just could not persevere, which was the end of the relationship. People are different. To one, "for worse" becomes an offense. They become unfaithful during times of trouble and even break the relationship to start a new relationship. While to some, "for worse" is a time to prove their heart of love and stay committed till the end of the struggle—like Dr. Glenn Mollette did. Truly, taking offense is a choice.

Reflection

1. Paul said, *"And herein do I exercise myself, to have always a conscience void of offense toward God, and toward men"* (Acts *24:16 KJV*). List ways you can exercise yourself against being offended.

2.   What are some benefits of living an offense-free life?

3.   The woman in Matthew 15 chose not to be offended. What were some things she did instead, and how can we apply her example?

CHAPTER 7

DO NOT GIVE ROOM TO THE DEVIL

When angry, do not sin; do not let ever your wrath (your

exasperation, your fury or indignation) last until the sun goes down.

Leave no (such) room of foothold for the devil (give no opportunity

to him). (Ephesians 4:26-27 AMPC)

Do you give room to the devil when offended?

You can give room to the devil in many ways when offended. However, I will mention a few.

Gossiping and Sowing Seeds of Discord

You give room to the devil when you are offended by gossiping. When people are offended, they often look for people to agree with them and take their side in the situation. They make sure they plant a seed of hate against the other person so the individual(s) they are talking to also hate the person who offended them.

God is not pleased with whoever goes around causing discord or division in the family, the church, the workplace, or the community. When someone is offended and decides to go around telling people things about and against the offender, it only worsens matters and may make reconciliation more difficult.

> These six things the Lord hates, yes, seven are an abomination to Him: A proud look, a lying tongue, hands that shed innocent blood, A heart that devises wicked plans, feet that are swift in running to evil, a false witness who speaks lies, and one who sows discord among brethren. (Proverbs 6:16-19 NKJV)

If you find a divided family or church, they are not without one or more persons who sow seeds of discord, whisper, and scatter. *Proverbs 16:28 says, "A perverse man sows strife, And a whisperer separates the best of friends."*

Refusing Dialog and Reconciliation

Navigating broken relationships requires discernment. While some benefit from reconciliation efforts, others find growth through amicable separation. Factors like mutual respect and willingness to resolve play crucial roles. Ultimately, the focus should be on fostering healing, growth, and mutual respect, whether through reconciliation or parting ways.

In relationships where dialogue is imperative for reconciliation, refusing to engage in conversation can worsen matters, giving room to the devil. By avoiding dialogue and reconciliation, issues may linger, leading to more problems down the line. Embracing open communication is key to resolving conflicts and preventing further discord.

Other ways of giving room to the devil are being resentful, developing hatred and bitterness, telling lies about the offender, and refusing to forgive. Some people prone to causing offense—especially gossipers—are always afraid of confrontation.

They want the listener to believe their story but do not like a dialogue setting aimed at reconciliation. They are afraid to be exposed, but concealing the truth only worsens matters and leads to broken relationships. Many have broken their relationships with divine helpers because of whisperers and scatterers.

Communicating the Offense to the Wrong Person(s)

You give place to the devil when you relate the story of the offense to the wrong person, who eventually gives you the wrong counsel. Your choice of words and the emotions you display also have a big role to play in complicating or resolving the conflict.

Here are things to look for to recognize the wrong person. The wrong person may take sides with you and magnify the offense, giving you reasons to be bitter or retaliate. The wrong person will be a tool in the hands of the devil to keep you in the bondage of unforgiveness. The wrong person will partner with you to sow more seeds of discord and scatter the relationship. The wrong person does not have the grace to resolve that problem and bring peace. The wrong person is carnal and void of a good understanding of God's Word.

The opposite of all these are attributes of the right person. It is essential for every child of God to discern the wrong person(s) and never involve them in matters of conflict. You may not speak to anybody except you have spoken to the offender. Only then might you need to speak to the right person. (See the Lord's prescription for reconciliation in chapter 9).

Listening to Bad Counsel

Sometimes, those who give unwise counsel have believed a lie from the first reporter. *Proverbs 18:17 says, "There are two sides to a story. The first one to speak sounds true until you hear the other side and they set the record straight" (TPT)*. So, you give room to the devil by listening to bad counsel when you are offended.

The wrong advice will make you even more angry and cause you to continually justify your anger. When you are angry, you must not look for people who will tell you what you want to hear; instead, go to people (counselors) who will tell you what you need to hear to diffuse the situation and help you heal.

When you are angry, you must not look for people who will tell you what you want to hear; instead, go to people (counselors) who will tell you what you need to hear to diffuse the situation and help you heal.

Resenting the Offender

You give room to the devil when you decide to resent, snub, dwell on the wrong, remain bitter, and refuse to confront the offender to dialogue (in a situation where dialogue is necessary).

If you decide never to have anything to do with the offender in a matter that requires reconciliatory talks, you are not helping your heart or the relationship.

Sometimes, there is a breaking apart that is healthy for your soul and destiny, and such separations may happen after an offense. For such a situation, the Holy Spirit, your godly counselor, will let you know. And when such a separation happens, you will have a pure conscience, peace, goodwill, and forgiveness, but never

bitterness or hatred.

Welcoming and Meditating on Wrong Thoughts

You give room to the devil when you welcome wrong

thoughts and begin to consider revenge. So, if you are offended,

don't sin, nor let the sun go down on your anger, or open doors for

the devil. Instead, allow the Holy Spirit to give you the grace to

overcome the evil one.

The offended person is always vulnerable to the devil's

attacks, especially in thoughts. The devil usually fights for the

opportunity to suggest things in the mind of the offended person. He

tells lies, brings arguments, and emphasizes reasons for continuous

anger and possible revenge. He brings wicked imaginations to mind.

He keeps the offended meditating on the wrongs of the offender day

and night. At night, the offended may have little or no sleep, and if

they sleep at all, they soon awaken with thoughts of the offense

flooding their minds.

When the devil speaks to the mind of the offended, he speaks using the first-person singular, deceiving them to believe they are the ones thinking. Knowledge of God's Word and a willingness to please God will help at this point because the offended person will be able to identify the whispers of the devil and be willing to ask the Holy Spirit to help their thoughts.

If you are offended, it is a conscious and deliberate decision for you to make. You must make a choice because your mind, at this point, has become a battleground. If you welcome evil thoughts and wicked imaginations, the next thing will be to make wrong conclusions and decisions. Whatever thoughts and imaginations you welcome in your mind when you are offended will determine your mood, decisions, actions, behavior, character, the final outcome of the offense, and eventually, your fate and eternal destiny.

Child of God, whenever you find yourself in such a situation, ask the Holy Spirit to help you. Ask for the grace to fight the good fight of faith because Jesus has already given you the victory, and you just need the grace to manifest it. Rise up immediately, and pray in line with these Scriptures:

> For though we walk in the flesh, we do not war after the flesh: (For the weapons of our warfare are not carnal, but mighty through God to the pulling down of strong holds;) Casting down imaginations, and every high thing that exalteth itself against the knowledge of God and bringing into captivity every thought to the obedience of Christ. (2 Corinthians 10:3-5 KJV)
>
> Finally, brethren, whatsoever things are true, whatsoever things are honest, whatsoever things are just, whatsoever things are pure, whatsoever things are lovely, whatsoever things are of good report; if there be any virtue, and if there be any praise, think on these things. (Philippians 4:8 KJV)

Refusing to Forgive

The subject of unforgiveness is treated more extensively in chapters 12 and 13.

When you make up your mind not to forgive, you are hurting

yourself because that is exactly what the devil desires for you. The devil will do everything to harden your heart so that you do not decide to forgive. He knows that unforgiveness makes you a candidate for hell, no matter how prayerful you may be or how much you serve God.

Refusing to forgive is giving room for the devil to enforce darkness in and around you; it is your spiritual imprisonment. Child of God, understand that forgiving your offender is not doing them a favor. Instead, you are doing yourself a huge favor, and God is pleased.

What You Must Watch for When You Are Offended

Matthew 26:41 says, "Watch and pray, that ye enter not into temptation: the spirit indeed is willing, but the flesh is weak" (KJV).

Sometimes, the sin of the offended becomes more grievous than the initial offense—the offender's sin. So, when you are offended, you must watch your thoughts, words, actions, and imaginations. You must watch who you communicate your hurts to, the places you choose to go to at that moment, and the decisions you make.

One could make very bad decisions when angry, only to regret after. Many decisions made during anger have hurt many relationships and ruined them.

The Bible tells us to think of things that are lovely, honest, true, praiseworthy, and of good report, but this is not usually the case when someone is angry. Because the devil brings bad thoughts into your mind against the offender to keep you continuously angry and even bitter, asking the Holy Spirit to help you at that moment can change the story from bad to good.

The Bible tells us to watch and pray so we do not fall into temptation; this does not just mean some random external enemy. It also refers to watching what is happening in our hearts and minds.

Reflection

1. This chapter lists several ways we can give room to the devil. Which one(s) pose the most challenge for you and why?

What adjustments can you make to practice avoiding these ways? To whom can you be accountable?

2. Why must you watch who you communicate your hurts to, the places you go when offended, and your decisions? What consequences might ensue if you don't?

CHAPTER 8

OFFENSE HAS WEIGHT AND POWER

The power of offense is destructive.

O ffense has power because it is a sin. Sin has power; therefore, it is important to understand that offense has power. *Romans 6:6-7 and 10 says, "We know that our old sinful selves were crucified with Christ so that sin might lose its power in our lives. We are no longer slaves to sin. For when we died with Christ we were set free from the power of sin" . . . When he died, he died once to break the power of sin. But now that he lives, he lives for the glory of God" (NLT).*

If an offense is not properly handled, it has the power to torment and enslave. An offense can drive away sleep from your eyes and keep you tormented for as long as you let it. Offense has the power to upset one's thoughts and mood. The moment you are offended, the devil sees it as an opportunity to bring bad thoughts into your mind, which may eventually upset your mood and decisions. Offense can have a negative influence on one's behavior. If someone is resentful and acts awkwardly consistently for a prolonged period because of offense, it could result in a change of character and the breaking of valuable relationships.

Prolonged offense has broken an untold number of relationships all over the world. It is the cause of many divorces in the world today. Offense has shattered families, and many children are suffering today because of broken homes.

Offense has the power to bring pain and suffering. Offense has the power to bring bitterness, hatred, and death.

Many people suffer from depression because of offenses. In ninety-five percent of the counseling that I have done, the parties came offended with each other, and in most of the cases, one or both counselees were depressed before counseling. Grunlan and Lambrides said, "Depression is a widespread phenomenon. Many therapists find that people with depression dominate their caseloads. As we get actively involved in lay counseling, we will find ourselves, sooner or later, dealing with depressed persons."[15]

Some people have murdered others because of offense, and some have committed suicide because of offense. Offense has imprisoned people and changed their destinies for the worse. Offenses have the power to complicate themselves, where one offense can birth about ten more offenses, resulting in a chain of offenses. It has the power to influence decisions that can negatively affect individuals, families, cities, communities, states, nations, and many generations to come. Offenses have possibly sent some people to hell.

The devil is the one who enforces the power and grievousness of offenses. The devil not only enforces the power of offense but also hardens people's hearts, so they do not forgive their

---

[15] Stephen Grunlan and Daniel Lambrides, *Healing Relationships: A Christian's Manual for Lay Counseling* (Eugene, OR: Wipf & Stock, 2005), 122.

offenders. But we thank God for Jesus Christ, who has overcome the devil on our behalf and breaks the arms of the wicked. *"For the arms of the wicked shall be broken, But the Lord upholds the righteous" (Psalm 37:17 NKJV).*

So, those who choose not to let offense prevail will yield to the Holy Spirit and experience the grace to handle offenses correctly and stop its chain of grievous events. They will choose to yield to the Holy Spirit and receive the grace to manifest godly power over the evil power of offense by forgiving and releasing the offender from their hearts.

Mercy Achu said, "We were never designed to live in a state of unforgiveness."[16] This is because unforgiveness is one of the key factors of broken relationships and the miseries accompanying it. When I say offenses have the power to send people to hell, it is because if the offended does not forgive the offender, the offended

---

[16] Mercy Achu, *The Formidable Power of Agreement* (Latavia: Empowerment Book Publishers, 2019), 55.

will not also be forgiven by God and eventually will go to hell.

The weight of offense can be unbearable.

Offenses have weight because offense is sin, and the Bible describes sin and the troubles it brings as a heavy burden. That is why Jesus calls for everyone with a heavy burden to come to Him and have rest (Matthew 11:28).

> Wherefore seeing we also are compassed about with so great a cloud of witnesses, let us lay aside every weight, and the sin which doth so easily beset us, and let us run with patience the race that is set before us. (Hebrews 12:1 KJV)

Depending on the gravity of an offense or how grievous the offense is to an individual, you may hear them say words like "The offense is heavy in my heart," or "It's very painful," "I can't bear it," or "My heart is heavy." The weight of an offense depends on how the offended perceives the offense. It is often spoken of as the degree or level of offense (or simply, how bad the offense is), but it has much to do with the stance of the offended.

The gravity of the offense may also determine the degree of hurt, intensity of anger, and subsequent actions. How much you allow the offense to be heavy on you may also determine how grieved, hurt, or angry you become because of the offense.

What will weigh much on someone else's heart, making them feel hurt, humiliated, or completely broken, may mean little or nothing to another person if the same thing were done to them. People are different. They reason differently and react to offenses differently. This could be based on their different cultures and values, how much of God and God's Word they have in them, and how close they are to God.

I have heard people say, "Oh, they spoke words that made my heart heavy." That's because of the impact of the words that were spoken. They were not encouraging but destructive. Just from hearing offensive words from a person, people break down into tears because the words negatively impact them. No wonder the Bible says, *"Death and life are in the power of the tongue, And those who love it will eat its fruit" (Proverbs 18:21, NKJV).*

Brace Up for Offenses

Bracing up for offenses and determining to follow peace can reduce its impact on you. It is important to make a conscious and deliberate decision to follow peace with everyone.

> Pursue peace with all men, and the holiness without which no one will see the Lord, watching diligently so that no one falls short of the grace of God, lest any root of bitterness spring up to cause trouble, and many become defiled by it. (Hebrew 12: 14-15 MEV)

If not well handled, one offense can cause a chain of offenses that can defile many and break up many relationships. However, as a child of God, if you brace up for offenses, choose not to take offense, and rely on the Holy Spirit to give you the strength to do what is right, you can save many relationships and lives, including yours.

When you are getting into marriage, a new workplace, a new environment, or a new community, or you find a new friend, you may expect offenses. Hence, it is important to brace up for offenses ahead of time because getting to know and acquaint yourself with new people, new relationships, and a new environment takes time.

In the process, offenses may occur. If you already have this in mind, you will not be shocked when offenses come, and your early or preparatory prayers will prevent a lot of bad circumstances and save you from a lot of pain.

An Opportunity to Know Me

In as much as an offense can by itself be very painful, people also experience pain from the resulting separation or broken relationships. An offense can be one of those bad experiences that occur to reveal you to yourself. So, taking a stance that with every offense, you would like to know what you can learn from it and become better could be another way of bracing up for offenses. This stance could positively influence your reactions when there is an offense against you. Note what John Maxwell said about reactions.

How do you usually respond to bad experiences? Do you

explode in anger? Do you shrink into yourself emotionally? Do you detach yourself from the experience as much as possible? Do you ignore it? John McDonnell once said, 'Every problem introduces a person to himself.' What an insight! Each time we encounter a painful experience, we get to know ourselves a little better. Pain can stop us dead in our tracts. Or it can cause us to make decisions we would like to put off, deal with issues we would rather not face, and make changes that make us feel uncomfortable. Pain prompts us to face who we are and where we are. What we do with that experience defines who we become.[17]

This is so true because you can only know that you are a very angry person when situations that cause anger occur, and such situations are most likely offenses. With a positive stance, you can become a better person after every offense.

---

[17] John Maxwell, *The 15 Invaluable Laws of Growth: Live Them and Reach Your Potential* (New York: Center Street, 2012), 121.

Reflection

1. Sin has power, and an offense is a sin. Therefore, offenses have power or weight. What are some things offenses have the power to do, and have you seen these things in your life or family background?

2. How and why do offenses have the power to lead people to hell?

3. What does it mean to 'brace up for offenses,' and what benefits does doing so yield?

4. How has God used offenses to show you yourself? What did you learn?

CHAPTER 9

HOW TO HANDLE OFFENSES

Steps to Reconciliation

Forgiveness is an obligation in the restoration of every troubled relationship. The Word of God says that offenses must surely come. Therefore, you must depend on the Holy Spirit to help you live a life of continuous forgiveness so that your God-ordained relationships will thrive and be blessed in a world with many problems. So, for the believer, forgiveness is an obligation, not an option. Mercy Achu says:

> Forgiveness is not an option, if you are not willing to forgive, please don't waste your time to pray. No matter how hurt you are, choose to forgive. Cry out to God and say, 'Father, I choose to forgive. Take away the pain of the hurt.' Jesus came to heal the brokenhearted (Luke 4:18). He heals the

brokenhearted and bandages their wounds (Psalm 147:3 NLT).[18]

When you are offended, it is very important that you follow God's way for reconciliation. With the help of the Holy Spirit, you can always make room in your heart to forgive. On your own, it may sometimes be difficult to forgive, but the Holy Spirit is an amazing helper. The prescription for handling offenses (reconciliation) that will be mostly discussed here is for the born-again believer in Christ Jesus, who is likely also a member of a local church. I call it a prescription because Jesus Christ is our Great Physician. He heals the brokenhearted with the medicine of His Word and in ways we cannot fathom.

Here are some essential steps in God's way for reconciliation:

1. *Talk with the person privately (one-on-one dialogue).*

---

[18] Mercy Achu, *The Formidable Power of Agreement* (Latavia: Empowerment Book Publishers, 2019), 55.

"Now if your brother sins against you, go and tell him about his fault between you and him alone. If he listens to you, you have gained your brother" (Matthew 18:15 MEV). When someone offends you, the first step is to go to them. It's important to know that you, the one who is offended, should initiate reconciliation. Some people can offend and behave as though they never did anything wrong. Confront the person. This type of confrontation is not to make war, but it should be for peace and reconciliation. It is to make the offender aware of what they have done, which you believe is wrong.

Sometimes, people can offend you unknowingly, meaning they are not aware that they have offended you. So, the first step is always to talk to the person concerned and no one else. Speak with them and express your desire for peace and reconciliation.

When confronting that person, do so with a loving and gentle attitude. Do not be harsh, rude, or mean. It will be better if you pray before meeting the person. The Bible says, *"Let your speech always be with grace, seasoned with salt, that you may know how you ought to answer each one" (Colossians 4:6 NKJV).* This works for married couples, friends, work colleagues, church members, siblings, neighbors, and all relationships. Dialogue is powerful. It enables people to understand each other and sheds light on the way forward.

Proverbs 15:1 says, "A soft answer turns away wrath, But a harsh word stirs up anger" (NKJV). So, a lot of the success of this confrontation lies in how you approach it and your attitude during the conversation. Many times, if you approach the situation in a kind and gentle way, the person readily apologizes, and the problem is quickly solved.

It's a sign of maturity when people own their shortcomings and take responsibility for what they did or said wrong. A person who values a relationship, fears God, and is willing to pursue peace can decide to apologize, even if they think they were not wrong. In this case, they apologize because they understand the other person is hurt. The words "I am sorry" can quench the fire burning in a hurting heart and be the last words to end the problem.

2. *Have a neutral third party mediate.*

Sometimes, going to talk to the offender can be very challenging. Some people hardly own their mistakes. They are self-righteous, proud, and arrogant. There are always such people all over. They always claim to be right, and meeting them for reconciliation could be like increasing the flames with more fuel. God knows this very well, so He gave us the next step to follow in the reconciliation process. *"But if he does not listen, then take with you one or two others, that by the testimony of two or three witnesses every word may be established"* (Matthew 18:16 MEV).

If the person did not respond accordingly the first time you went and spoke with them, or the issue was not solved, or they refused to listen, the next step is to bring in one or two people to come along with you to solve the problem. Third parties need to be neutral and not have a bias for you or the other person involved. This person(s) needs to have good judgment and should be able to judge wisely and bring light and understanding to the problem. Sometimes, it's good to bring another person in because they may see things differently and may explain things better than you. Listening to a third party may help the offender to understand better and be open to reconciliation.

The third party should be a trustworthy person or a counselor you trust. When the matter is being deliberated on with a third party, talk solely of the issue. Do not be harsh with your words, and try not to attack the offender. It is not a time to win an argument but to reconcile and restore a peaceful relationship. For any offender, saying the words "I am sorry" is very powerful in healing the relationship.

3. *Bring it to the church.*

"If he refuses to listen to them, tell it to the church; but if he refuses to listen even to the church, let him be to you as a Gentile and a tax collector" (Matthew 18:17 MEV). If you have spoken to the person privately and they refused to listen to you, then you bring in a third party, and they still don't listen to them; the next and final step is to escalate the issue and bring it to the church's attention. This

third step is drastic but necessary. Taking it to the church does not

mean that you grab the mic one Sunday morning and put the person

on blast in front of the whole congregation. It simply means you take

the issue to your local church leadership so that they can step in and

try to solve it.

The idea here is that if the offender did not listen to you and

did not listen to the mediator you brought in, they would at least fear

the church leadership and quickly resolve the issue. The church

leadership represents God here on Earth. So, in a sense, it prompts

this person to at least let the fear of God push them to reconciliation

or making peace. Bringing it to the church is also a public testament

in the presence of God and man that you are intentional about

reconciliation and peace, are willing and have gone through all the

correct avenues to pursue that peace. If it still is not resolved, the

Bible says that you have been absolved of any guilt and

condemnation concerning the issue (in the sight of God and man)

and to treat that person as if they were a pagan. This doesn't mean

you treat them badly; it means their actions have shown they are not a true child of God (because a true child of God seeks a resolution and peace). And so, you treat them like you would any unbeliever. You forgive the person and love them, but set reasonable and healthy boundaries for yourself.

It is important to note that if you and the offender do not belong to the same local church, the heads of your biological family will be okay to handle the matter following step three if you are related. Or, if you are colleagues at work, you can talk to the heads of the establishment or follow the establishment's protocol for handling complaints or offenses. The most important thing is that you forgive.

When resolving a conflict, watch out for these things:

- A self-centered response. Watch out for self-justification and self-vindication. Avoid the tendency to blame and fight. It's self-examination and reconciliation time, not fighting time.
- Acting clueless as if you don't understand why the other person or persons are offended.

- Attacking people's personalities instead of focusing on the problem. It's unacceptable.

- The inclination to withdraw in response to conflict. Refrain from succumbing to avoidance, apprehension, or fear of confronting the offender. Additionally, resist the urge to retaliate by ignoring them. Retaliating in response to wrongdoing involves stooping to the level of the offender or seeking revenge.

If someone offends you but refuses to apologize, you are still required to forgive them. Your forgiveness is not contingent on the other person's repentance. Your job is to forgive regardless. Some people will never apologize for the wrong they did to you and will never admit their wrong. That doesn't mean you'll live the rest of your life in anger and bitterness. You forgive them anyway. No matter how hard it is, God will always strengthen you and give you the grace to do the right thing if you are willing.

Reflection

1. Matthew 18:15 says we should first speak to the person who offended us directly and not to anyone else. Why is this sometimes hard to do? What are the benefits of doing this?

2. How can you avoid being defensive if someone is courageous enough to tell you that you offended them? What else should you avoid and why?

CHAPTER 10

WHEN YOU FIND IT DIFFICULT TO FORGIVE

God can easily forgive, but it's not usually so with us human beings. Sometimes, forgiving is a struggle, especially when you find it difficult to forget the offense. But God forgives and forgets and remembers our sins no more.

We all need help from the Holy Spirit to forgive and forget. God has promised in His Word to help us. He is our Father. He understands our frailty and shortcomings. That is why He says in *Isaiah 41:10, "Fear not, for I am with you; Be not dismayed for I am your God. I will strengthen you, Yes, I will help you, I will uphold you with My righteous right hand" (NKJV).*

God is willing to help you whenever you are having difficulty forgiving. He has given you the grace to forgive and still wants you to ask Him for help whenever you feel that you need it.

He doesn't ask you to do what you are unable to do.

Be honest with God.

Before you get help, come to God in prayer and be honest with Him. If you are not willing to forgive, tell Him the truth. He already sees your heart. There is no need to pretend. Ask for the grace to be willing to forgive. If you are willing to forgive but unable to forgive, probably because the memory of the offense still makes you feel hurt and angry against the offender, tell God just as it is and ask Him for the grace to be able to forgive and forget. Ask the Holy Spirit to root out every hurt and plant the seed of forgiveness in you. Linn and Linn address the potential freedom the Holy Spirit's help brings.

> By asking the Spirit to root out any hurt and to plant God's forgiving love, we are choosing to stop being slaves and to start becoming freed men. We are expressing our willingness to surrender to Him hurts that have controlled us and to grasp the Spirit whose love fills us with power to freely

act...Though the Spirit can remove immediately the anger or resentment of the painful memory and replace the hurt with God's love, He usually moves gradually as we cooperate by forgiving.[19]

The Seed of Forgiveness

So, upon your request, the Holy Spirit sows the seed of forgiveness in you, and you receive the grace to forgive and forget. The Holy Spirit is the one who heals your heart from hurt. For some people, healing of the hurt can be a process, and for some, it can be immediate. You can open your mouth, tell the offender you have forgiven them, and continue a lifestyle of intimacy with God. The lessons you learn from the experience can be life-transforming, and you can help others in the future. Mercy Achu shares her own experience, saying:

Every time somebody hurts me, I just go to God and cry, 'I

---

[19] Dennis Linn & Matthew Linn, *Healing of Memories: Transforming Past Hurts into Gifts.* (New York: Paulist Press, Inc. 1974, 1984), 31.

choose to forgive, Father help me; take the pain away.' I may have to do that a couple of times, but I have purposed in my heart that no human being born of a woman, will cause me to lose my place of fellowship with the Father and perhaps even miss heaven in the process. Beyond having your prayers go unanswered is the broken fellowship with the Holy Spirit, why would you allow that. I have heard it said; unforgiveness is like drinking poison and wishing another person died. Let us not allow unforgiveness to rob us of our inheritance in Christ Jesus.[20]

Reflection

1. How can being honest with God help you forgive? How can honesty with God about your weaknesses strengthen your fellowship with Him?

---

[20] Mercy Achu, *The Formidable Power of Agreement* (Latavia: Empowerment Book Publishers, 2019), 55.

CHAPTER 11

IN DANGER OF HELL: MY TURNING POINT

1st Testimony: I Struggled with Unforgiveness

This testimony explains how I was unable to forgive until the Holy Spirit helped me. In my early years as a young pastor's wife, I had little or no experience. My husband started pastoring as an assistant pastor in a local church, and I worked with him. I observed the elderly in the church and learned from them. I was part of the intercessory group and made sure I was always present for Bible studies because I needed to grow spiritually.

As a new believer in Christ and a pastor's wife, I wasn't prepared for any personal offenses. It hadn't fully registered with me that I had embarked on a journey requiring additional strength, wisdom, and grace from God. I was quite naive, believing that everyone in the church was entirely focused on Jesus and loving each other. I never imagined there could be intentional hurt or offense among us.

Then, one day, a fellow Christian offended me deeply, and I felt a surge of anger and hurt. It was particularly painful because I had left behind my unbelieving friends who engaged in cursing, lying, gossiping, and betrayal. I had entered a community of godly people, expecting not to encounter such behavior anymore. The disappointment was compounded because I had hoped for better conduct from a fellow believer.

In my anger and ignorance, I tried to imagine how to get revenge but arrived at nothing. Then, I concluded that God would take revenge on my behalf. The sun went down on my anger many days, and I did not know I was displeasing God.

I thought that God would sympathize with me.

I justified my feelings by reasoning that I was the one who had been wronged, not the one who had wronged another. Therefore, I believed God must be on my side, sympathizing with me. I confronted the Christian, who admitted his mistake, and I thought I had forgiven him. However, I found myself disappointed every time I saw him and avoided speaking with him. Deep down, I still harbored a sense that he deserved some form of retribution for his behavior.

In that condition, I attended a women's meeting and was given a front seat as they normally did for pastors' wives. The speaker was also a pastor's wife who had just flown in from another country. To my surprise, her message was about forgiveness. While she was teaching, I asked God, "Lord, do you mean that I am now the sinner simply because I have not forgiven? Don't you see that the other person was wrong, and I was right?" I almost got offended with God for using this lady to emphasize forgiveness. As she continued teaching, I felt more hurt because it seemed like God was now holding me responsible instead of sympathizing with and comforting me. I felt like God should have said, "My daughter, don't worry. I know what you are going through, and I will deal with those who offend you. I've got your back."

In Danger of Hell if You Don't Forgive

Instead, the teaching was that I was in danger of going to hell if I did not forgive from my heart. It did not make sense to me, so I really felt bad and did not know what to do. I felt like God had taken sides with my offender. But as the teacher expounded more on God's Word, I began to reason, especially when she made it clear that Jesus came for us when we were still evil because He loves us. She said no matter the offense, God requires that we forgive because He has forgiven us of many sins. This is how I know the Holy Spirit is a wonderful person; He still patiently ministered in my heart, even though I had a struggle in my heart.

If You are Not Willing to Forgive . . .

The speaker spoke something that touched my heart (I am paraphrasing): "If you are not willing to forgive, be honest and tell God that you are not willing to forgive, and ask for the grace to be willing to forgive." Then she went on: "Or if you are willing to forgive, but you are not able to forgive, ask the Holy Spirit to sow the seed of forgiveness in your heart." I had never heard anything like that—to ask the Holy Spirit to sow the seed of forgiveness in me.

I'd rather forgive than go to hell.

At this point, I told myself that I did not want to go to hell; I would rather pray, as she said. So, I prayed and told the Lord that I was willing to forgive, but I was not able to, and I wanted the Holy Spirit to sow in my heart the seed of forgiveness. At that moment, my thoughts changed. I realized a new trend of thoughts flowing in my mind; that the devil is my enemy, not my Christian brother. The devil caused him to betray me so that I could be at loggerheads with my brother. My mindset towards that brother began to change.

My brother is my brother; the devil is the devil.

In my mind, I saw him as my brother and the devil as the devil. In just a moment, my heart and my mind changed. It was as if a major shift caused a certain darkness to disappear from my heart. In an instant, I began thinking to myself that the devil is the wicked one, and he is the brain behind the offense.

Peace with God and Man

My mind shifted from blaming man to blaming the devil; then, love flowed in my heart toward my brother in Christ. While I was still in this mood and meditating, the speaker said, "Now, tell the Lord that you have forgiven, and forgive from your heart." So, I immediately told the Lord I had forgiven from my heart.

My mind shifted from blaming man to blaming the devil.

Immediately, I felt the peace of God and joy in my heart. I realized I had just received healing for hurting, and my joy had been restored. There was such peace in my heart that I could not explain. It was an amazing experience.

After the conference, I went to the brother again and told him I had forgiven him. Maybe he was surprised because he did not know I had not completely forgiven him. Thank God, I forgave and received my peace with God and man.

The Holy Spirit is our helper. Call on Him when you are offended and hurting; He will help you to forgive and replace your hurt with healing if you let Him.

2nd Testimony: I Suffered False Accusation and Separation from a Friend

This second testimony explains the importance of dialogue when there is an offense. Dialogue is very important whenever there is an offense between married couples, friends, church brethren, siblings, or colleagues at work. Dialogue gives the opportunity to express one's mind and understand the reasons for actions and words that caused the offense.

I was upset with my friend, but I wanted a reconciliatory meeting.

I had a very good friend whose name I will not disclose. For confidentiality, I will give her a different name, Abta. Abta was a pastor's wife, and we were friends for many years. Abta had a new friend, whom I will call Dikie, for confidentiality reasons.

One Sunday after church service, Abta approached me in anger, accusing me of saying something I hadn't. She claimed someone had told her I had slandered and spoken ill of her behind her back. I was taken aback and asked her who had given her this information, but she refused to reveal the source. I insisted that she tell me so that we could confront the person together and resolve the misunderstanding.

I knew the allegations were all false. But I realized Abta believed the allegations were true. I was upset because I had been friends with Abta for many years, and I did not expect her to believe something about me without verifying it. In addition, I had never backstabbed her. I told her that, as a true friend, she should tell me who gave her such a report so that we could sit and talk, but she totally refused.

I was really offended because I did not know how to proceed to resolve the matter. Plus, she believed a lie against me, and there was no agreement to dialogue for me to defend myself. I also did not know who told my friend the lie. I was so hurt because I told myself we had been friends for so many years, and suddenly, a fabricated story separated us in minutes.

So, I decided to pray. I cried to God and told Him that He knew I was not guilty. I asked the Lord to reveal the person who told a lie to Abta against me.

A whisperer separates chief friends.

I also told Abta that because she decided to believe a lie against me and was not ready to bring the person so we could talk, she and that person would cease to be friends, and of course, our friendship ended too. The whisperer separated us. I couldn't trust Abta from that point onwards.

I asked God to give me the grace to forgive. I forgave Abta, but we were not as close as before because of a lack of trust.

A perverse man sows strife, and a whisperer separates the best of friends. (Proverbs 16:28 NKJV)

God convicts the whisperer (answered prayers).

After several months, my husband and I were sitting in the living room when we heard the doorbell ring. When I opened the door, it was Dikie, Abta's new friend. Dikie came in and went on her knees, sobbing and pleading for our forgiveness. We asked her what the matter was and why she was asking for forgiveness, but she continued sobbing and could not explain anything.

After a while, she said she had spoken a lie to Abta against me. She said that ever since she told that lie, she had no rest, everything was falling apart, and nothing was working for her. She really wept and said she believed that God was punishing her for fabricating a lie against God's servant. I was surprised, and we all marveled at how God brought this to light. At that moment, I remembered that I had prayed that God should reveal the person who told the lie to Abta so that Abta would truly know that I was innocent. And God did it.

I had the grace to forgive, and I forgave.

What God did was amazing to us. Immediately, while Dikie was still speaking, we called Abta, and with Dikie's permission, we put the phone on speaker. Dikie openly apologized to Abta and to us for telling her a lie about me. Wow! That was a big miracle because I had never seen a thing like that. So, in my mind, I was wondering, "Hmm, now that Dikie has repented and apologized openly, what will Abta do with all the words she threw at me for no reason?" The truth is that Abta became ashamed.

I was ready for us to dialogue and restore our friendship, but she was not ready. I visited Abta to let her know I was no longer offended with her. In addition, I was excited that God had intervened on my behalf. However, she was not ready for any conversation relating to the issue.

Some months passed by, and her husband visited from overseas and gave us a call. During that call, he made an appointment to meet with us. Abta and her husband, as well as my husband and I, had a meeting during which we discussed the matter honestly, resulting in Abta finally apologizing to me. The friendship was restored, but total healing and rebuilding of trust was in progress.

God helped us. We all experienced total healing not long after, and Abta went to be with the Lord a few years later. The dialogue played a very big and positive role. There was a better understanding after the dialogue.

This issue taught me how a whisperer can truly separate true friends. The experience also taught me that God cares about our relationships._He is pleased when His children are living in peace and harmony. Thank God for the grace for reconciliation.

Reflection

1. Why does unforgiveness put believers in danger of hell? Why might offenses be one of the devil's trusted weapons against believers?

2. Has a whisperer ever affected any of your relationships? How can we avoid the detrimental effects of whisperers?

CHAPTER 12

IDENTIFYING BITTERNESS & UNFORGIVENESS

Bitterness can reveal itself in various forms. Quite often, you may not even know that you are bitter from an offense until a lot of time has passed and great damage has been caused. In the same way that you can't see the roots of a tree growing in the ground, it may be hard to identify bitterness because it is a root.

It's a root in your heart that goes with deceit. Yes, with deceit, because you could tell yourself that you have forgiven, only to later find yourself complaining bitterly against the offender when something comes up that relates directly or indirectly to the old offense. Or, you could have a sudden change of mood when the offender you claim you have forgiven shows up where you were not expecting to see them. So, anyone who is not honest will deceive themselves that they have forgiven when they have not truly done so.

A root is a source or bubbling fountain lying underneath the surface. Roots do not directly manifest themselves.

The Root of Bitterness

Hebrews 12:15 says, "See to it that no one fails to obtain the grace of God; that 'no root of bitterness' springs up and causes trouble, and by it many become defiled" (ESV). The Bible likens bitterness to a root that can spring up and cause trouble enough to pollute or stain many souls.

A root is a source or bubbling fountain lying underneath the surface. Roots do not directly manifest themselves. Roots are a source of nutrition and fuel for other elements that are on the surface. It's just a matter of time before the outward manifestation reveals what is hidden beneath the surface. Lou Priolo calls bitterness the root that pollutes:

Roots have to be planted. So let me ask you, What do you suppose is the seed that, when planted in the soil of our hearts, sprouts into a root of bitterness? Generally speaking, it is a hurt. When someone hurts you, it is as if that person dropped a seed of bitterness onto the soil of your heart. At that point, you can choose to respond in two ways. Either you can reach down and pluck up the seed by forgiving your offender, or you can begin to cultivate the seed by reviewing the hurt over and over again in your mind. Bitterness is a result of dwelling too long on a hurt.[21]

When you manifest signs of bitterness, and it is brought to your attention, you may pretend that you are not offended and say everything is fine. Yet when you see, hear, or think about your offender, you feel something negative in your heart towards them. But you pretend and convince yourself that you are not mad and are okay. This is not a root you need to neglect, and it must be dealt with accordingly before it completely overtakes and destroys your life.

Bitterness arises from holding onto unforgiveness. When your responses to an offender are improper or not in line with

---

[21] Lou Priolo, *Bitterness: The Root that Pollutes* (Phillipsburg, NJ: P & R Publishing, 2008), 7.

biblical teachings, it signals bitterness. Bitterness acts like poison to the soul of the one who harbors it. Lou Priolo said, "The verb translated 'to be bitter' means 'to cut' or 'to prick.' You may think of bitterness as an internal, self-inflicting wound, and so it is. Bitterness is the result of not forgiving others."[22]

This is not a root you need to neglect, and it must be dealt with accordingly before it completely overtakes and destroys your life.

How can you know that you are bitter?

You know you are bitter when:

- You find yourself manifesting self-centeredness and self-defense, claiming that you are right and secretly brooding in anger. Also, having a victim mentality, forming a pity party, and having your mind preoccupied with negative thoughts about the one you are offended with.

[22] Ibid., 6.

- You withdraw and intentionally avoid someone who has offended you by giving them the "cold shoulder." It can also be seen as a form of vindictiveness.

- You become intolerant, you are unable to put up with the offender, cannot face the person, or can't stand being around them.

- Your heart is thinking of vengeance, or you are exercising acts of vengeance and retaliation by gossiping, slandering, making spiteful remarks, or backbiting the offender.

- You find yourself constantly criticizing, condemning, and portraying judgmental attitudes, impatience, or disrespect.

- You are in rebellion, especially against authority—rebellion can hardly occur without bitterness.

- You notice that you're easily upset or reacting strongly to minor things as if they were major offenses; it could mean you've been holding onto past grievances.

What other things can be seen in someone who has refused to forgive?

An Unpleasant Atmosphere

The atmosphere around someone who is bitter and angry all the time is rarely pleasant. They may always be complaining. The dark energy that comes from unforgiveness attracts many evil spirits. Those evil spirits then bring several other things that follow this person around. The following can also be noted:

- Pride

- Arrogance

- Suppressed anger

- Pretense/hypocrisy

- Outbursts

- False accusations

- Pity party attitude

- Sarcasm

- Slander

- Afflictions

- Pain

- Rejection

- Depression

- Disease

- Suicide—untimely death

- Homicide

Haughtiness and Arrogance

If you speak to the person who offended you with haughtiness and arrogance, treating them as inferior, like a child, or dismissing their significance, it reveals bitterness.

Anger and Overreactions

It is a sign of bitterness if you find yourself having outbursts of anger and overreacting emotionally. Sometimes, bitterness might pop up in an ugly way like blowing up at people unjustly because of the accumulation of the record of wrongs or doing something bad in anger to prove you are angry. Watch out for these outbursts. If you are experiencing these, it shows that you are bitter and have not forgiven the one who offended you. Don't retaliate. God does not want His children to retaliate because He says vengeance belongs to Him, and He will pay back. When you identify bitterness in your life, it is time for you to seek help. It's time for you to speak out, and be sure to speak out to the right people. Hurry, because you are in danger.

Reflection

1. This chapter lists ways you can know you are bitter. Review them. Is anything on the list happening in your life? Are there signs of unforgiveness?

2. Bitterness is like poison. How can you avoid consuming this deadly drink?

CHAPTER 13

CONSEQUENCES OF UNFORGIVENESS

There are several grievous consequences of unforgiveness. The following list is of paramount importance.

1. **God will not forgive you.**

    Matthew 6:15 says, "But if you do not forgive men for their sins, neither will your Father forgive your sins" (MEV).

    - The Bible says that if you do not forgive, God will not forgive you. How do you expect God to give you something that you are not willing to give to somebody else?

2. **God even calls you wicked when you refuse to forgive others.**

    Matthew 18:32 says, "Then his master, after he had summoned him, said to him, 'O you wicked servant! I forgave you all that debt because you pleaded with me. Should you not also have had compassion on your fellow servant, even as I had pity on you?" (MEV).

- You may magnify the offense and justify your reasons for not forgiving, but you must remember that you sin against God, offending Him daily. And despite your shortcomings and sins, He is always willing and eager to forgive you. And because He does that for you, He wants you to extend that same grace to those who have offended you. According to Mercy Achu, "Unforgiveness will sap the joy of living in your life; it will literally incapacitate you. Your thinking becomes distorted and the more you hold on to it, your heart feels like it's taken on a hundred pounds."[23]

- Unforgiveness is a load of sin, a burden which you, the

---

[23] Mercy Achu, *The Formidable Power of Agreement* (Latavia: Empowerment Book Publishers, 2019), 55.

offended, are carrying, in addition to the hurt from the offense. So, it's important to get the burdens off you, at least one after the other. You can start by putting off the load of unforgiveness, and you will find grace in the sight of God for the healing of the wounds that you had from the offense.

3. **Your prayers will not be answered.**

Refusing to forgive the one who offends you is disobedience to God's Word, and the Word of God calls you wicked. *". . . You wicked servant! I forgave you. . ." (Matthew 18:32 NKJV).* How, then, can your prayers be answered? The same way God reacts to the wicked when they pray to Him is the same way He will react to you. *"Then they will cry out to the Lord, but He will not answer them; He will hide His face from them at that time, because they have wrought evil deeds" (Micah 3:4 MEV).*

- Your prayers to God will be unanswered because you are living in disobedience and rebellion toward Him; He has instructed you to forgive, but you have not obeyed Him.

How do you expect God to answer your prayers if He is not pleased with you? *"Behold, the Lord's hand is not shortened, That it cannot save; Nor His ear heavy, That it cannot hear. But your iniquities have separated you from your God; And your sins have hidden His face from you, So that He will not hear" (Isaiah 59:1 NKJV).*

- How do you expect Him to move on your behalf if He is not happy with you? Unforgiveness hurts you, not your offender, because it hinders your prayers and stands as a wall between you and your blessings. Forgive so that it may be well with you.

4. You will be under oppression (a spiritual prison).

- Unforgiveness opens the door to tormentors and oppressors (evil spirits), which afflict your life. Unforgiveness goes hand in hand with anger and bitterness. Demons love being around people who are bitter and angry because those dark emotions are a suitable environment for evil spirits.

- Evil spirits thrive in environments that are gloomy and tense. The more you dwell in those feelings and emotions, the more demons hang around you. And those demons bring their own curses and bondages, and they pull you into a deeper and darker place. *Matthew 18:34-35* says, *"In anger his master handed him over to the jailers to be tortured, until he should pay back all he owed. This is how my heavenly Father will treat each of you unless you forgive your brother or sister from your heart"* *(NIV)*.

- These prisons are usually enforced by demonic forces to place you under torment. That is why you feel drained when you spend time with a negative person. It's the spirits around that person that drain your spirit.

- Evil spirits do not like a joyful atmosphere and will find it difficult to inflict a pure-hearted and joyful person. So, let go of unforgiveness so that you can get out of the spiritual prison that comes with unforgiveness.

- When you refuse to forgive, you are open to tormenting thoughts that can keep you restless and take away your sleep. That is a prison situation where you lose your sleep and keep meditating in anger over an offense. In such a situation, your soul could be dark and vulnerable to demonic attacks of ill health, accidents, and many evils. Why? Because you have broken your hedge of protection.

5. **You will have stress and a lack of peace.**

- Some people develop stress, and consequently high blood pressure, because of the stress they get from constantly meditating on the offense and the offender. If you refuse to forgive, you make yourself ungodly. And your heart will remain heavy, and you will be stressed. *"There is no peace, says the Lord, for the wicked" (Isaiah 48:22 NIV).* Unforgiveness takes a huge toll on your body. It feels heavy, and it is a huge burden to carry around every day.

- Have you ever noticed that when you see someone who

has offended you or even heard their name, it changes your mood and affects the way you talk, act, or do other things? Most times, you cannot even be free around this person. Sometimes, you cannot look at them in the eyes or even be around them because of how negatively it affects you when you are in their presence or even think about them.

- Think about how miserable you are when you are angry with someone you care about. It could be your spouse or a close friend. You are unhappy and miserable until you make peace with them.

- Our bodies are not meant to hold onto negative emotions such as bitterness and unforgiveness. When we experience these emotions, it often leads to discomfort and unhappiness. This discomfort serves as a signal from our bodies, urging us to release these emotions because they are not beneficial for our well-being.

- You may be sick physically because of bitterness, but your perception may be clouded, and you may not see it. So, you may attribute the sickness to other things, but the root cause is unforgiveness. We must delete all files of bitterness (both past and present) from our lives and ask God to make us whole again.

- Unforgiveness can greatly affect your life and prevent you from having a great quality of life. It is something that affects your well-being mentally, emotionally, and physically. In the end, it hurts only you.

- There are no benefits of unforgiveness. Let go of unforgiveness so your body can begin to heal itself. Let go and let God have His wonderful way.

6. **Unforgiveness will cause you to lose good relationships.**

- Bitterness, unforgiveness, and resentment do not create a conducive atmosphere to cultivate good and lasting friendships. So, you will lose good relationships because of that.

- The feelings that you carry because of unforgiveness will start manifesting in your current relationships. Because you are bitter, you may be bitter to your loved ones (transferred aggression) whether the offense was from them or not.

- You will have difficulty trusting people because of past betrayals and past hurts. You may not see the good in your present relationships because of your past hurts.

- You may even unconsciously punish your loved ones for the sins of the offender, and that takes a huge toll on a relationship.

- You can seek help from a counselor, deal with any leftover trauma from any relationship that brought you pain, and ask God to heal you completely. If not, you will make others pay for the crimes of the offender.

- You may hinder yourself from bringing great and meaningful people into your life because you may sabotage those relationships due to the bitterness and anger you carry with you. Not everyone will hurt you as that person did. Forgive and make room in your heart so

God can bring in new relationships.

- The moment you start living in unforgiveness, you cease being in fellowship with God. Our relationship with God is the most important one we must cherish. We must ensure that nothing stands between us and God, our Father. He is love. He demonstrated His love for us while we were yet sinners by sending His only begotten Son to come to this sinful earth and die for our sins, set us free from the slavery of the devil, and give us eternal life. So, if He loved you while you were still a sinner who did not merit His sacrifice of love, then you also ought to forgive those who offend you, even if they do not see their wrong and apologize. So, not only do you break your relationship with those you refuse to forgive, but you also break your relationship with God. God, in His mercy, will keep coming after you (through His Holy Spirit) to restore His fellowship with you by convicting you to forgive your offender. This is because His mercy endures forever.

- However, if you harden your heart and never forgive your offender until you leave this world, then you will have a broken relationship with God forever as you go to hell.

7. **Unforgiveness is a stronghold that hinders the blessings of God.**

- Unforgiveness can mess up the flow of your life in many areas. You are not walking in the favor of God when you are unforgiving.

- If the Scriptures call the one who refuses to forgive his brother "wicked," then with your unforgiving heart, whatever is allotted for the wicked is also your portion.

- The Bible says God is angry with the wicked every day. How can you expect to receive God's favor for His blessings of breakthrough and open doors when your heart is wicked?

- You are walking under a closed heaven. Some blessings that could come to you will be hindered because you have closed the door.

- Unforgiveness can be a barrier that can close your finances, cause stagnation in your business or many areas of your life, and cause people who were willing to help you not to help you anymore.

- Unforgiveness can prevent you from shining, hinder your productivity, and prevent your divine helpers from locating you. Divine helpers are sent by God to you to help you accomplish your purposes in life or arrive at your destiny.

- When you refuse to forgive, and you let the root of bitterness grow in your heart, you create a dark spiritual atmosphere around you. Demons are in this dark spiritual atmosphere, as I mentioned earlier.

- You are walking in darkness, and because of that, you can stumble and fall.

- There is no love where there is unforgiveness, and if there is no love, there is hatred. So, unforgiveness gives birth to hatred. *"He who loves his brother abides in the light, and there is no cause for stumbling in him. But he who hates his brother is in darkness and walks in darkness, and does not know where he is going, because the darkness has blinded his eyes" (1 John 2:10-11 NKJV).*

- How can it be well with you when God is not pleased with you? How can it be well with you if you are walking around with an atmosphere that attracts evil spirits? Evil spirits don't bring blessings. They bring bondages, yokes, setbacks, and curses.

- Since you have refused to forgive, you have given the evil spirits the legal ground to mess up your life. For the sake of your peace and prosperity, let go of unforgiveness so that it may be well with you.

- God desires above all things that you may prosper, but that can't happen if your life is not in alignment with His will. We walk in God's favor when we please Him. And being obedient to God's Word in the act of forgiveness makes God pleased with you. *"When a man's ways please the Lord, He makes even his enemies to be at peace with him" (Proverbs 16: 7 NKJV).*

8. It destroys the offended person's life in the long run.

- Unforgiveness, as I mentioned earlier, takes a huge toll on your physical body. But apart from that, it can also ruin other areas and facets of your life. The type of person you become due to bitterness can ruin your life in the long run.

- Someone related a story to me of two ladies whose hearts were broken by men when they were in their 20s, and those women held on to that betrayal throughout every relationship they went into. They are now single and bitter in their 50s and 60s, still singing that same song of bitterness, even to their children, influencing them negatively. If those women had just dealt with that unforgiveness when it happened, they could have eventually ended up in beautiful, meaningful relationships. They would have had a better quality of life. Instead, they are still single and bitter over something that happened when they were in their 20s.

- Many children today who face underlying issues often have parents who did not effectively address offenses or manage their own unforgiveness. Consequently, some of these unresolved emotions were transferred to their children, significantly impacting their emotional well-being.

- Unforgiveness can ruin your life and the lives of those around you.

- You may find yourself constantly reviewing hurtful mental images that may eventually lead you to a state of depression and psychosomatic illnesses. It's sad to say, but most of the people who offend you go on to live happy lives, and you are left to deal with the pain they caused.

- Your refusal to forgive them may not affect their lives in any way, but it ruins yours. Someone once described unforgiveness as preparing poison for someone else and then consuming it yourself, hoping to harm the other person. You only hurt yourself in the process. Don't let it rule your life. I understand it is painful, but ask God to give you the grace to forgive and let it go.

9.   It gives the devil free access to your life.

The schemes of the devil are what make us to be at odds with one another. *". . . if there was anything to forgive—I have forgiven in the sight of Christ for your sake, in order that Satan might not outwit us. For we are not unaware of his schemes" (2 Cor 2:10-11. NIV).*

- If Satan loves one thing from you, it is for you to stay angry when offended. He wants this because this is one of the ways he can gain access to your life. And once he comes in, he comes only to steal, kill, and destroy. Do not give him that opportunity. Resist him, and he will flee from you. Forgive your offender and shut Satan out of your life, out of your destiny path, and out of your household.

10. You no longer walk with God. You are walking in darkness.

"This then is the message which we have heard from Him and declare to you: God is light, and in Him is no darkness at all. If we say that we have fellowship with him, yet walk in darkness, we lie and do not practice the truth. But if we walk in the light as he is in the light, we have fellowship one with another, and the blood of Jesus Christ His Son cleanses us from all sin" (1 John 1:5-7 MEV).

- God is light, and in Him, there is no darkness. If you are going to walk with God, you cannot walk in darkness or carry around anything that breeds darkness, and that includes unforgiveness.

- If you choose to walk in unforgiveness, you have chosen to walk in darkness, and if you walk in darkness, you are not walking with God. That means that God is not with you, and you are not in fellowship with God.

- Those who walk in darkness do not know where they are

going because there is no light to light their path. If you

are walking in darkness, you may be living your life in

reverse, going the wrong direction, making the wrong

choices, having setbacks, and making decisions that will

harm you in the long run.

- Unforgiveness is the mother who gives birth to

   bitterness. You will not perceive the things of God clearly

   because you are walking in darkness. Let go of

   unforgiveness and receive God's light so God can guide

   your life. You are in better hands when you walk with

   God and live daily in fellowship with Him.

11. You are deceiving yourself. If you die, you will go to hell.

James 1:20-22 says, "Because human anger does not

produce the righteousness that God desires. Therefore, get rid of all

moral filth and the evil that is so prevalent and humbly accept the

word planted in you, which can save you. Do not merely listen to the

word, and so deceive yourselves. Do what it says" (NIV).

- Unforgiveness is a sin—plain and simple. It does not

matter how much you justify the hurt and pain the person caused you. God understands and acknowledges your pain. Yet, the responsibility still lies with you to forgive, trusting that God will handle the rest.

- Bitterness clouds perception and understanding and opens someone to deception. If you don't forgive and die in your unforgiveness, you will go to hell. Unforgiveness is a deadly sin and may cost you your eternal life if you do not repent of it.

Reflection

1. This chapter listed several grievous consequences of unforgiveness. Are there indications of any of them in your life? What can you say to God to ask for His help in reversing any of these consequences?

CHAPTER 14

MUST I RECONCILE WITH THE OFFENDER?

When I forgive someone, must we continue to walk together?

"Do two people walk hand in hand if they aren't going to the same place? (Amos 3:3 MSG)
"Do two people walk together, if they have not agreed?"
(Amos 3:3 MEV)
"Can two walk together, unless they are agreed?" (Amos 3:3 NKJV)

Forgiveness and reconciliation are not the same. Forgiveness means you pardon your offender; you let go. Reconciliation means restoring a broken relationship to what it used to be, or even better, reuniting and walking together once more.

Reconciliation is often seen as the final step in the forgiveness process. Forgiveness and reconciliation can occur between the offender and the offended once the issue has been resolved, but this isn't always the case. Sometimes, forgiveness happens without reconciliation. However, it's typically challenging for reconciliation to occur without forgiveness, especially after an offense has occurred.

The Bible states that two cannot walk together unless they have agreed to do so. When you see two or more people who have had conflicts or offenses, resolved them, and are now moving forward together again, it demonstrates the power of agreement and unity among them. Otherwise, it is difficult for the two to walk together if they are not in agreement.

Forgiving someone doesn't automatically mean you have to continue the relationship. It's important to think about the nature of the relationship, too. Some relationships are destined, while others are not. I am certain that I am meant to be with my husband, to whom I have been married for forty-three years and counting. In our relationship, if we experience a conflict, we seek not only repentance and forgiveness but also reconciliation. This is because our relationship is of God; we love each other deeply and have decided to stay married for life. This also applies to others who are equally certain that their relationship is ordained by God for a specific purpose on Earth.

If you've recently moved to a new school and were warmly welcomed by a student who quickly became a close friend but later discovered they engage in gossip, lying, and are involved in mystical or dark practices which they concealed from you, it can be unsettling. If this person then offends you by gossiping, spreading false information, and betraying your trust, resulting in a conflict that requires intervention from the school counselor, the situation can be challenging. After the counselor settles the matter, you might forgive them but decide not to maintain a close relationship with them moving forward.

Some meetings intended to resolve conflicts and possibly bring people back together can become very complicated. This happens because some people never admit when they are wrong, no matter the effort, which relates to what the Lord said in *Matthew 18:17. "And if he refuses to hear them, tell it to the church. But if he refuses even to hear the church, let him be to you like a heathen and a tax collector" (NKJV).* And of course, it can also be difficult to walk with such a person if you also consider this Bible passage: *2 Corinthians 6:14-16 says, "Do not be unequally yoked together with unbelievers. For what fellowship has righteousness with lawlessness? And what communion has light with darkness? And what accord has Christ with Belial? Or what part has a believer with an unbeliever? And what agreement has the temple of God with idols? For you are the temple of the living God. As God has said: "I will dwell in them, And walk among them. I will be their God, And they shall be My people."*

If someone refuses to acknowledge their wrongdoing and apologize, it's wise to maintain distance. Show that you've forgiven them and have no intention of seeking revenge through your actions. Surprisingly, some people might react with even more anger and cause more trouble if you try to tell them you've forgiven them.

Going to announce your forgiveness to some people could be challenging.

If you've sincerely forgiven someone who has malicious intentions, it's important to seek guidance from God. Ask for wisdom to discern whether approaching them to say you've forgiven them is appropriate. Also, ask God for wisdom on how to set necessary boundaries with them.

When an offender shows that they are sorry for their wrong and improves their behavior, expressing forgiveness can be a positive gesture. However, it's crucial to do so with grace and dignity while setting clear boundaries to prevent further harm. Sometimes, meeting with someone to convey forgiveness can provoke more offenses, particularly if approached without wisdom. For instance, it would be unwise to go alone to visit someone who has assaulted you, perhaps sexually, to tell them that you have forgiven them. You can still forgive sincerely while prioritizing your safety and making prudent choices to maintain distance.

When God forgives humanity, He invites them to walk with Him according to His holy principles. God does not impose His presence but grants free will to choose a relationship with Him.

While God desires reconciliation with all, not everyone embraces His ways. For those who claim repentance yet live inconsistently, God sets a boundary, stating, "I will vomit you out." This emphasizes God's expectation for genuine repentance and steadfast commitment to His principles. *Revelation. 3:15-16 says, "I know your works, that you are neither cold nor hot. I wish you were cold or hot. So then, because you are lukewarm, and neither cold nor hot, I will vomit you out of My mouth" (NKJV).*

In conclusion, if you have purposed in your heart to live a godly life, and all you want to do is walk with God and please Him all your life, you will forgive every offender, but you will not reconcile with everybody. There must be separation from some people because they are scatterers, destiny destroyers, and dedicated servants of the devil, and you only get to know their true identity after an offense. Love, forgive, and move on with God with a clear conscience.

Reflection

1. In what circumstances is it wise to forgive but not reconcile? Why?

CHAPTER 15

WAYS TO AVOID BEING EASILY OFFENDED

A postle Paul said he "exercised himself against offense," and we can do the same (Acts 24:16). Here are some ways to avoid being easily offended.

Living a Lifestyle of Studying God's Word and Being Prayerful

- When you cultivate a lifestyle of prayer and reading and studying God's Word, you live a life of intimate relationship with God.

- You cause the presence of God to increase in your life continually. You are creating a godly atmosphere in your life; therefore, you will also experience the power of not unnecessarily taking offense.

- You will experience the ability to easily forgive when you are truly offended. Living a life of intimacy with God helps you overcome situations that could throw you down.

- The presence of God makes the difference. Being full of God's presence means being full of His Holy Spirit, and being full of His Holy Spirit means having the fruit of the Holy Spirit. Galatians *5:22-23 says, "But the fruit of the Spirit is love, joy, peace, patience, gentleness, goodness, faith, meekness, and self-control; against such there is no law" (MEV).* I can't imagine any offense ever happening if everyone had and manifested all the fruit of the Holy Spirit.

- Married couples who often pray together love themselves more, understand each other better and eventually have one mind because they are always in the presence of God together. Whenever you come before God in prayer, He does a good work in you.

- When couples and whole families study God's Word and pray together often, they stay in peace because they're inviting the presence of the Prince of Peace—Jesus Christ—in their midst. God's Word and prayer change people. There is transforming power in the Word of God.

- The closer you get to God, the holier you become; you become more like Him. And if you are like Jesus, you will not cause offense or wrongfully take offense. *"For God is the one working in you, both to will and to do His good pleasure" (Philippians 2:13 MEV).*

- You will not only forgive but also live a life of forgiveness if you are closely walking with God and have all the fruit of the Holy Spirit. You must develop a nature of love, compassion, and mercy towards others. Forgiveness comes from the heart of a new nature wrought in Christ. As you give yourself in complete surrender to God, you will experience a life of peace and victory by the power of the Holy Spirit.

- Your spirit man will experience strength to overcome as you pray, read, study, believe, and obey God's Word. Dr. Nicku

Mordi describes the benefits of intimacy with God:

> To become intimate with Him is to know how to spend time in your secret place, that is the place where you will be encouraged and inspired. You will always hear Him giving you advice on how to overcome your struggles or how to better succeed in whatever you are doing.[24]

- A life of prayer is very important if you want to handle offenses correctly and keep your relationship with God and your God-ordained relationships intact.

Make the moments of praying alone a very special and more enjoyable time—not for problem-solving time but enjoying Him. Be consumed with Him, and He will fill you with Himself. I promise you, instead of just existing, you will start to live differently. What now seems so difficult to bear will

---

[24] Dr. Nicku Mordi, *Never Forgotten* (Mustang, OK: Tate Publishing, 2012), 110.

not matter anymore. You will know it is part of life and your Father will help you go through because He watches over you always. Let it settle into your mind and into your spirit that you are important and you are never forgotten. Jesus also confirmed by saying, 'In the world ye shall have tribulation; but be of good cheer; I have overcome the world' (John 16:33). Indeed, be of good cheer, God will send help or a solution that you need at the right time.[25]

God has forgiven your many sins because he cherishes His relationship with you as a Father to His child. Whenever you ask God for forgiveness, He never hesitates to forgive you. The Bible says He is good, and His mercy endures forever. In the same way, you will choose to forgive those who offend you, first to please God and be at peace with Him and then the people concerned. And, of course, you will experience God's joy and peace within you whenever you forgive.

---

[25] Ibid., 109.

There is no human relationship that has not experienced offense in one way or the other. Since you have received forgiveness from God and continue to receive it repeatedly (recognizing imperfection), you should extend forgiveness to others consistently. As Jesus said, forgive seventy times seven.

There is no human relationship that has not experienced offense in one way or the other.

- As a believer in Christ, you have your own sins forgiven and are in right standing with God. You must obey God's Word and forgive everyone who offends you.

- When you pray for your friends, siblings, brethren, relatives, co-workers, classmates, and everyone you interact with, including your enemies, God will always take control of every situation. Many bad things will be prevented by your prayers. And if God allows anything that will offend you, it will always be for your good, for His glory.

Talk yourself out of that offense.

- When someone offends you, you have the choice to either succumb to the hurt and pain or to decide not to let it dominate your life and release it.

- Try to think rationally and critically about what happened. Ask yourself, "Is it even necessary for me to be angry? Did that person mean to hurt me? Did it happen as I pictured it in my mind, or am I taking it wrongly? What lesson is here for me to learn?" etc. Sometimes, doing it that way will help you realize that you were taking things more seriously than they were.

- It's important to remind yourself that not everyone thinks or feels the same way you do.

- Give the person who hurt you the benefit of the doubt and try to understand that they are entitled to their opinion and to think how they want to think. But they do not have control over your emotions. So, you can choose not to take offense to what they said or did.

- Remind yourself, "They have the right to say or think as they wish, but I have the right to protect my heart from offense, and I choose not to harbor anger."

Acts 24:16 says, "This being so, I myself always strive to have a conscience without offense toward God and men" (NKJV). The devil uses offense as bait to get believers to sin by being offended and not forgiving because he knows that through that means, he can have an opening to attack the believer. An angry and unforgiving person is vulnerable to the enemy's attacks of wrong ideas, sudden destructive decisions, and even spiritual attacks.

- So, you can trust the Lord to help you to stay free from offense. This takes spiritual exercise by being prayerful, studying the Word of God, and trusting and leaning on the Holy Spirit to help you manifest His fruit whenever needed. If you stay free from bitterness, you will stay in the will of God. If you become offended and decide to remain bitter, the enemy will take you captive to fulfill his own purpose and will.

- So, take your pick: Which will it be? It is better to stay submitted to God and resist the devil so that he flees from you, and you stay victorious.

- The dream or vision of your life will probably happen differently than you think it will, but His Word and promises will not fail. Disobedience is the only thing that can abort God's plan. Offense is a deadly trap; with this knowledge, you will do all the spiritual exercises necessary to help you not fall into that trap.

- Understanding that offense is a deadly trap gives you the determination to stay free from it. John Bevere describes this determination:

> It takes effort to stay free from offense. Paul compares it to exercising. If we exercise our bodies, we are less prone to injury. When we exercise forgiveness and refuse to take up offenses, we keep our consciences fit and clean. Sometimes, others offend us, and it is not hard to forgive. We have exercised our hearts so they are in the condition to

handle offense; therefore, no injury or permanent damage results. But some offenses will be more challenging than those we've been trained to handle. This extra strain may cause a wound or injury, after which we will have to exercise spiritually to be healed again. But the result will be worth the effort.[26]

- You may decide to thank God for the offense done to you by your friend, sibling, spouse, or in-law (whatever relationship you are encountering the offense from). This may be hard to do, but it is possible with the help of the Holy Spirit, and it works. *"Pray without ceasing, in everything give thanks; for this is the will of God in Christ Jesus for you" (1 Thessalonians 5:17-18 NKJV).*

- It may not make sense to thank God when you are hurting, but the Bible says we should give thanks to God in

---

[26] John Bevere, *The Bait of Satan, 20th Anniversary Edition: Living Free from the Dealy Trap of Offense* (Lake Mary, FL: Charisma House, 2014), 255.

everything. It is God's will that you thank Him for everything. At that moment when you begin to thank God, even if you are thanking Him in tears, He will respond to you with love and relieve the pain in your heart.

- Thanking and praising God when you are in pain is sacrificial and calls for the Holy Spirit's intervention. He will help you because He is our helper. He will remind you of God's Word, comfort you, inspire you to have the right thoughts, and give you peace. *Psalm 147:3 says, "He heals the broken in heart and binds up their wounds" (MEV).*

Meeting the healer before confronting the offender will change the course of the matter from bad to good.

Meeting the healer before confronting the offender will change the course of the matter from bad to good. Taking time to pray when you are offended can change the offense's outcome. As Christians, I believe this is what we ought to do, even before confronting the offender. For with God, all things are possible.

Try to understand the offender.

- If you try to put yourself in the other person's shoes and try to understand why they did what they did, it'll be easier to sympathize and forgive. I've noticed that when I make an effort to understand others, learning about their experiences and how those experiences have shaped them, it helps me empathize with them instead of becoming upset.

- Recognizing the pain and hurt that may underlie someone's anger, particularly if they offended me in a moment of their own anger, helps me forgive and release the issue. Considering their values, cultural background, age, gender, and temperament also influences how I approach the situation.

Anticipate offense.

- Here is an experience a family member had. She said, "When I was in college, a few of my friends hurt me so deeply. I wasn't sure if the friendship was going to survive. I called another friend who was like a spiritual mentor to me. I just needed some advice on how to forgive and whether I should continue the friendship or just close that door. I remember we were on the phone for over an hour. But the one thing he said that stood out to me till this day is this: "If you anticipate offense, you won't be so mad when it happens." I didn't quite understand what he meant until he explained it. He said, "We are all humans, and we are all full of flaws, and we all make mistakes."

- This is so true; as humans, we are bound to make mistakes occasionally, and because of that, people can offend each other anytime. It's not because they are bad people. It's simply because they are human. With that mindset, it's easier to forgive and extend grace to the offender because you understand that you also can make mistakes.

- When you recognize that everyone is imperfect and may offend you at times, you can anticipate potential offenses and let go of them before they affect you deeply.

- When you move to a new school to meet new schoolmates,

get into a new relationship, or meet new people for the first time and get to know them, anticipate offense and brace up for it.

Reflection

1. There is no human relationship that has not experienced offense in one way or the other, so we must avoid being easily offended. This chapter lists ways to do that. Which way have you practiced in the past, and what was the result?

2. What two ways from the chapter can you intentionally practice to improve one of your relationships over the next two months? Who can hold you accountable for working on this?

CHAPTER 16

MANIFEST THE POWER OF FORGIVENESS

Forgiveness is a force; to forgive is power being manifested because Jesus referred to the ability to forgive as having power. *"But that you may know that the Son of Man has power on earth to forgive sins–then He said to the paralytic, 'Arise, take up your bed, and go to your house. And he arose and departed to his house" (Matthew 9:6-7 NKJV).*

What is power?

- The ability or capacity to make things happen.

- Power is authority.

- Power is control and influence.

- Power is a force that can be manifested in words, actions, and thoughts.

- It is to dominate, command, and reveal strength.

- Power is an inherent characteristic of God.

What does it mean to forgive?

- To pardon, cancel a debt, or acquit.

To forgive is a deliberate decision to release the feeling of vengeance and resentment towards an offender or offenders and let go of any claim to be compensated for what was lost or suffered by the offended.

All power belongs to God. He is the Almighty Creator. Only God has the power to forgive an offender and let him go without a charge. Man receives the power to forgive only from God.

- Forgiveness is a force. It has power—it is powerful.

- Sin has power. *"It is sin that gives death its sting and the law that gives sin its power. But we thank God for giving us the victory as conquerors through our Lord Jesus, the Anointed one"* (1 Corinthians 15.56-57 TPT).

- But holiness is more powerful than sin. *"Come worship the Lord God wearing the splendor of holiness. Let everyone wait in wonder as they tremble in awe before*

Him" (Psalms 96:9 TPT)

- *"Then I will show how great I am. I will prove that I am holy. Many nations will see me do these things, and they will learn who I am. Then they will know that I am the Lord" (Ezekiel 38:23 TPT)*. Holiness has power. God is holy; that's why He is all-powerful. He is omnipotent. There is no sin in Him that can weaken Him.

- God is holy, and because of the power of His holiness, the devil trembles before Him. He cannot stand the power of God's glorious holiness.

There is no sin in Him that can weaken Him.

So, forgiveness, which is part of God's character, is more powerful than unforgiveness. Unforgiveness is a sin and a weight that can imprison you, keeping you in bondage. However, forgiving others will liberate you from prison. Forgiveness is a powerful and very important word in the kingdom of God. It's a vocabulary in bold print because that is the reason Jesus came to this earth; that is the reason Jesus died—that we may be forgiven.

Forgiving is the demonstration of the power of God.

- It is the demonstration of the power of holiness.

- The one who is holy has authority and subdues.

When you forgive:

- You are standing in agreement with God.

- You are on the side of holiness.

- You are exercising power and authority over sin. You are saying, "I have subdued the sins of hatred, bitterness, and unforgiveness. I am above them; I am stronger than them."

By so doing, you are manifesting the power of God inside you.

A sinful soldier is a weak soldier.

- Because sin weakens, unforgiveness weakens.

- With unforgiveness in your heart, you cannot rebuke the devil.

- With sin in your life, you are vulnerable to diabolic attacks.

- But holiness comes with spiritual strength and righteous authority.

---

*Holiness comes with spiritual strength and
righteous authority.*

Consider the more important factor.

"In every relationship be swift to choose peace over competition, and run swiftly toward holiness, for those who are not holy will not see the Lord. Watch over each other to make sure that no one misses the revelation of God's grace. And make sure no one lives with a root of bitterness sprouting within them which will only cause trouble and poison the hearts of many" (Hebrews 12:14-15 TPT).

- Consider what is more important and choose it.

- Peace is more important than offense.

- You should choose the more important factor.

- It is more important for you to follow peace than dwell in offense.

To forgive is more important to you and your destiny than unforgiveness. Choose what is more important to you, your soul, and your destiny, and ask for grace or the power to do it. God has the power to give you. Love is more important than hatred, and so is peace than strife. Unity for the course that pleases God is more important than separation that causes the devil to rejoice. Forgiveness will bring unity, while unforgiveness will bring separation.

As believers and soldiers of Christ, the most important person in our lives is our Lord, Jesus Christ, who is worthy of all honor, glory, and reverence. If anything is important and good to Him, then it must be important and good to us. What is important and pleasing to our Lord Jesus is forgiveness instead of unforgiveness. Therefore, that should be the more important thing for us.

Reflection

1. This chapter states that choosing to forgive is choosing to be on the side of holiness. Do you agree and why?

2. Why is forgiveness the more important factor?

CHAPTER 17

BENEFITS AND BLESSINGS OF FORGIVENESS

Everything we do has benefits or bad consequences. As a child of God, when you do what God has instructed you to do, there is always a blessing attached to it. The same goes for forgiveness. Living a life of forgiveness is not an easy thing to do, but if you do, here are a few of the benefits you will enjoy.

God will forgive you.

"For if you forgive men their sins, your heavenly Father will also forgive you" (Matthew 6:14 MEV).

- This statement is simple but impactful. You can't receive favor from someone who has not forgiven you or someone who is angry with you. If your boss is upset with you, you might miss out on a promotion opportunity because of the strained relationship. Conversely, being on good terms with your boss could increase your chances of being considered for promotion when the opportunity arises.

- God can show you favor and give you breakthroughs, prosperity, and many open doors when He is pleased with you. He will not withhold anything good from those who fear Him and do His will.

- He will even make your enemies to be at peace with you. When your enemies are at peace with you, they will cease to make evil schemes against you. They will stop striving with you. They will stop provoking you to anger simply because they are at peace with you by God's divine command. Consequently, you will be at rest.

You will receive the blessings of obedience.

"Great blessings belong to those who work to bring peace. God will call them His sons and daughters" (Matthew 5:9 ERV). "He will bless you at all times in everything you do" (Deuteronomy 28:6 ERV).

- God will reward your obedience and bless you. There are specific blessings that come to you only when you choose to obey God.

- Obedience sometimes can come from a place of sacrifice. That is why God rewards those who choose to make this sacrifice.

You will have open doors, and God's favor will be upon you. When you confront your offender for the purpose of peace and reconciliation, you have become the peacemaker, the initiator of reconciliation and peace. *Matthew 5:9 says, "Blessed are the peacemakers, for they shall be called the sons of God" (MEV).* You will be called the son of God, identified as God's own, as one who has God's own nature or characteristics in him. It's a blessing to be identified with God.

Forgiveness brings peace and deliverance.

- When you forgive, you will experience the peace of God within you, and God will also help you find peace within your heart towards the person who offended you.

- You will be well emotionally because your mind is no longer troubled by the offense, the thought of the offense, or the offender. *3 John 1:2 says, "Dear friend, I pray that you may enjoy good health and that all may go well with you, even as your soul is getting along well" (NIV).*

- Your sins will be forgiven, and you will have peace with God as a result. Just being in right standing with God is a place of peace and satisfaction. *"Blessed is the one whose transgressions are forgiven, whose sins are covered" (Psalm 32:1 NIV).*

You can experience healing in your body.

- Some people brought a paralyzed man to Jesus for Him to heal. When Jesus saw the man, the first thing He said to the man was, *"Son, be of good cheer. Your sins are forgiven you" (Matthew 9:2b MEV).* In their hearts, certain Scribes who were present accused Jesus of blasphemy. *"Jesus, knowing their thoughts, said, Why do you think evil in your hearts? For which is easier, to say, 'Your sins are forgiven*

you' or to say, 'Arise and walk'? But that you may know that

the Son of Man has authority on earth to forgive sins – then

He said to the paralytic, Arise, pick up your bed and go into

your house" (Mathew 9:4-6 MEV).

- If this paralytic was having a grudge in his heart against
  someone, he could not have been forgiven. He could have
  remained in his paralytic condition. Jesus decided to forgive
  him first. Perhaps his sins were responsible for his
  condition, so the Lord had to clear that out of the way for
  the man to be made whole.

- Holding onto resentment and not forgiving is sinful and
  could prevent physical healing. When you live in love and
  forgiveness, your physical body and health prosper because
  your body thrives in an environment of positive emotions.

- The stress caused by bitterness fades away the moment you
  forgive, and your body begins to heal from any physical

ailments caused by holding onto unforgiveness.

Forgiveness leads to the purification of your spirit.

"If we confess our sins, He is faithful and just and will forgive us our sins and purify us from all unrighteousness" (1 John 1:9 NIV). Unforgiveness goes hand in hand with many other dark emotions (bitterness, anger, jealousy, envy, pride, etc.), so when you choose to forgive, you are not only removing unforgiveness from your life, but you are also removing these other things that entered your life because of unforgiveness.

- Forgiveness opens the door for God to purify and cleanse your soul and spirit, freeing you from negative and dark emotions.

Forgiveness leads to healthier relationships.

- Making forgiveness a habit allows your relationships to grow and flourish. When all these negative emotions and bad habits that came because of unforgiveness are gone, the door opens for the relationships in your life to flourish.

- Just as a plant without sunlight will die, so will relationships that aren't fed with the light that comes from a pure heart and a clean spirit.

- When conflicts are resolved, the offense is dealt with, and there is reconciliation and forgiveness, the parties concerned learn many lessons and have a better understanding of the way forward. Because they want the relationship to continue, they know better what to guard against and how to relate to each other concerning the circumstances that caused the previous offense.

- For many, there is a new and good understanding, and life becomes better. Some may no longer need to walk together, but they have found peace with each other.

Forgiveness leads to a spiritual connection with God.

- When you forgive, your fellowship with God is restored. You can grow closer to God without any hindrance between you and Him because you are doing His will.

- When you are in God's will, you have access to His throne room to worship and fellowship freely with Him without any hindrance.

Forgiveness leads to freedom.

- When you forgive, even if you do it out of obedience to the Lord, you will find incredible power and freedom within. Bitterness is like a mental prison and a heavy burden to carry.
- Forgiveness is freeing in every way. Dr. Fondong describes it this way:

Forgiveness is the first gift the Father expects you to give to those who hurt you. It is an act of your will in obedience to the Father and a response to the forgiveness we have received from God. Forgiveness is the act of choosing to continue to receive God's forgiveness. Forgiveness is the notice of release you serve to your tormentors and prisoner wardens.[27]

---

[27] Dr. Elizabeth Fondong, *Freedom from the Spirit of Rejection: Receiving the Father's Love, Rejecting the Enemy's Lies* (Amazon Digital Services LLC, 2021), 85.

In Matthew 18:34-35, the Word of God explains that as the unforgiving servant was cast into the prison by his master, in the same way, your heavenly Father will cast you into prison to tormentors if you do not forgive the trespasses of others. So, forgiving one another is staying free from spiritual prison and spiritual tormentors.

God will lift you up.

- When you're hurt and angry, you might feel like retaliating or showing off to protect your pride. Your flesh tells you that you shouldn't allow anyone to humiliate you in such a way. So, you may feel your ego is crushed, and instead of approaching your offender to tell them how you are feeling, you stay away, resent them, or do some form of retaliation to make them know that you are important and deserve respect.

- So, forgiveness is an act of humility. God's Word says that God resists the proud but gives grace to the humble. It is an act of humility when you approach the offender for the purpose of reconciliation, forgiveness, or peace. God gives you grace, and He will lift you up. *James 4:10 says, "Humble yourselves in the sight of the Lord, and He will lift you up" (NKJV).*

Reflection

1. This chapter lists several benefits of forgiveness. Which benefits did you experience when you forgave? How do the benefits of forgiveness outweigh the grievous consequences of unforgiveness?

2. What part does humility play in forgiving?

CHAPTER 18

WHAT ABOUT THE OFFENDER?

"Therefore if you bring your gift to the altar, and there remember

that your brother has something against you, leave your gift there

before the altar, and go your way. First be reconciled to your

brother, and then come and offer your gift" (Matthew 5:23-24).

If your brother has something against you, you are considered the offender. God will not even accept your gift if you have offended somebody and are fully aware of it but do not care to ask for forgiveness, yet you are carrying a gift or offering to give God. Instead, God wants you to show love to the one you have hurt by going to say, "I am sorry," before bringing Him an offering. If you care so much about God that you want to give Him an offering, God prefers that you show that "caring" first to your brother whom you see and have offended by making sure that you relieve him of the pain you caused him before bringing your gift to Him (God).

As much as the one offended has the responsibility to forgive, the offender has the responsibility to repent of their wrong or apologize for their wrongdoing. The Word of God in *Hebrews 12:14, which says, "Follow peace with all men, and holiness, without which no man shall see the Lord" (KJV),* is for both the offender and the offended.

As much as the one offended has the responsibility to forgive, the offender has the responsibility to repent of their wrong or apologize for their wrongdoing.

- If you offend someone, do not stay quiet as if nothing has happened. God expects you to own your wrongs and take positive action toward reconciliation. Go meet the person and say, "I am sorry."

- Every offender has a conscience, except for someone whose conscience is seared. When you are aware of your offense, yet you are not willing to make peace, you lose your own peace, too. Your conscience troubles you.

- You break your fellowship with God and the one you offended. Life is not the same for you, too.

- Some offenders want to pretend that all is well and wait until the offended makes a complaint. Still, they are not able to fool their consciences.

- Some people are chronic, perpetual offenders and have placed themselves in the category of the wicked. *Isaiah 48:22 says, "There is no peace, saith the LORD, unto the wicked" (KJV).*

- There are some people who take pleasure in causing offenses. They are not happy to see some people happy; they are always devising wickedness, and their thoughts are continually evil. *"Evil shall slay the wicked: and they that hate the righteous shall be desolate" (Psalm 34:21 KJV).* This is the reason why the offended should not seek revenge because God will handle the offender.

- Therefore, no one should boast when they offend someone. If you offend and are aware, fear God and run quickly to make peace. Let your heart and mouth easily say, "I am sorry."

- When you offend someone unknowingly, maybe your spouse, friend, church member, fiancé, co-worker, neighbor, sibling, etc., it is important to admit your fault to the person the moment you are made aware.

- And if you offend knowingly, it is important to put yourself in the place of the person hurting. Some people find it difficult to own their wrongs. But it is helpful for you if you ask yourself, "How would I feel if someone did or said this same thing to me? What would I have said or done differently that would not offend? How can I contribute to solving this matter?"

- Someone who fears God and has a good heart will ask

himself questions such as those mentioned above. *Proverbs 9:10 says, "The fear of the Lord is the beginning of wisdom, and the knowledge of the Holy One is understanding" (MEV).*

- If you know God, you will understand His will and fear Him reverentially. And if you fear Him, you will be wise enough to do His will. Some people have offended others and never cared to apologize. They chose to be defensive to the end.

- If you love God and people, you will admit your faults and apologize when you do wrong. It is not wise to ignore the fact that the other person is feeling hurt because of what they believe you did wrong to them. Whether they are wrongfully or rightfully taking offense, you must face the issue as a real problem that needs to be addressed.

- Also, accept the reality about yourself and your friend, spouse, sibling, or whoever it may be.

- If you offend someone and it comes to the point where the

offended person desires that you both see a counselor, it is good to go because that could be a learning process for you to make you a better person.

- And when you attend counseling, your communication should be geared towards resolution and reconciliation, not defensiveness and trying to portray yourself as the winner.

- Be mindful of the fact that that problem may be an opportunity for you to exercise love, concern, honesty, and sincerity, and the relationship may get better after that issue is resolved. Even if you never walk together again, your life can still improve because the issue has been resolved, and valuable life lessons have been learned.

Reflection

1. This chapter explained that as much as the one offended is responsible for forgiving, the offender must repent of their wrong and apologize for their wrongdoing. Do you need to repent and apologize to anyone you have offended?

2. What steps can you take to ensure you properly handle

    offenses when you are the offender?

CHAPTER 19

WISDOM FOR PEACEFUL LIVING

Human nature often avoids admitting wrong and is slow to seek reconciliation, but as a child of God, having a heart of humility and love is important. Fear God and do what is right. Avoid causing offense and quickly admit your fault because it shows your integrity.

Here is some important scriptural advice to avoid holding onto offenses and to pursue a peaceful lifestyle with everyone.

- Confess and apologize for the sake of peace and reconciliation.

- As far as it depends on you, try to live in peace with everyone.

- Avoid situations that provoke offense and deal wisely with people who are faultfinders.

- Learn how to walk away from certain conversations.

- Sometimes, it is better to lose an argument but win the person and keep your relationship.

- Not everything needs to be addressed openly; the secret things belong to God.

- It's not necessary to continue to talk about the offense. *Proverbs 17:9 says, "He who covers a transgression seeks love, but he who repeats a matter separates friends" (MEV).* Once you forgive, do not keep bringing up the matter, for that alone can break the relationship.

- Seek peace through God's Word, even if the other person never apologizes. Place your trust in God's grace to forgive and move forward.

- Prayerfully set healthy boundaries. Not every person is good to be your friend or close collaborator. There are destiny helpers and destiny destroyers.

- Learn not to take certain things too seriously. Lean not unto your own understanding.

- Declare your forgiveness for others.

- You must not only forgive once, but you must also live a life of forgiveness. You must develop a nature of love, compassion, and mercy towards others. Forgiveness comes from the heart of a new nature from our Lord Jesus Christ.

You must not only forgive once, but you must also live a life of forgiveness.

- When you are offended, watch your words and your thoughts. Also, be mindful of who you are open to about that offense. When you speak to the wrong people, they will influence you negatively by speaking words or making comments that will stir up anger in you, causing you to be more offended. It's important to talk to people who can help defuse the situation and guide you towards forgiveness. Avoid confiding in friends prone to drama; instead, seek out mature individuals who can provide wise, godly advice.

- Also, make sure that you do not make any important decisions when you are offended. Some people have made reckless decisions when they were offended, and that has ruined several lives. If you must make any decisions, wait until you calm down. Give room for some time to pass. Time has a way of influencing many things positively, in addition to playing a positive role in the healing process. Take the time to think through the situation carefully before making a decision. This can help you avoid making regrettable choices.

- Remember not to give room to the devil by gossiping or accepting wrong suggestions. Giving room to the devil can cost your relationship. *Proverbs 16:28 says, "A perverse man stirs up conflict, and a gossip separates close friends" (NIV).* Gossiping about the offender, from person to person, will never restore the relationship. It could lead to permanent, regrettable separation.

- Do not plan revenge because, if it is necessary, God says He is the one to avenge us. *Romans 12:19 says, "Don't try to get revenge for yourselves, my dear friends, but leave room for*

God's wrath. It is written, 'revenge belongs to me; I will pay

it back, says the Lord" (CEB).

Implementing these tips can significantly impact both personal and professional relationships, as well as improve your emotional and physical well-being. You can also enhance your spiritual, physical, and emotional health, fostering the creation of positive relationships once again.

Reflection

1. This chapter listed scriptural advice to avoid harboring offenses and embrace a lifestyle of peace with all men. What are three pieces of advice you can implement over the next three months?

CONCLUSION

The Bible is correct in stating that conflicts are inevitable in relationships. Every relationship encounters challenges. However, applying biblical principles from this book can greatly influence how you handle these conflicts and whether your relationships endure.

Some relationships end due to conflicts and offenses, while others grow stronger after facing them. Not all relationships are meant to last, so conflicts or offenses can lead to their permanent breakdown. However, relationships that are meant to endure can thrive with the joint effort of those involved, even after an offense.

Relationships can improve after resolving problems and addressing offenses. The parties involved may discover more about each other, gain new insights, develop patience, and strengthen their love for one another.

In every relationship, God should be given first place because He is love, and only He gives true love, which covers a multitude of sins. If God is given first place, He keeps the relationship intact because He is the only one who can help us properly handle offenses.

ABOUT THE AUTHOR

By the grace of God, Dr. Mercy Forlu is a distinguished figure known for her unwavering dedication to both healthcare and ministry. With over four decades of experience as a Registered Nurse, she has tirelessly served the medical needs of communities since 1981. As the CEO, founder, and Director of Nursing of Grace and Mercy Health Services, established in 2002, she has extended healthcare assistance to underserved populations in Washington, DC, and Maryland. Additionally, she founded Grace and Mercy Community Services in 2022, focusing on providing mental health services to those in need in Maryland.

Beyond her illustrious career in healthcare, Dr. Mercy Forlu has left an indelible mark in ministry. Since her conversion to Christianity in 1978, she has achieved notable milestones:

- Diploma in Biblical Teaching, Southwest Bible College,

Limbe, Cameroon

- Certification as a Public Speaker, Teacher, Coach, and Trainer, The John Maxwell Team, Florida, USA

- Bachelor's degree in Pastoral Leadership, Indiana, USA

- Master's degree in Christian Counseling, Indiana, USA

- Ph.D. in Christian Counseling, Indiana, USA

- Honorary Doctor of Divinity, Maryland, USA

Dr. Mercy Forlu's leadership and commitment to advancing the kingdom of God are evident in her roles as:

- Vice National Women's Leader, Full Gospel Mission Cameroon (1996 - 2000)

- Visionary and Founder of Women for Jesus (WFJ) (1999 to date)

- Organizer of the Prophetic Possession March for Cameroon with WFJ (1999)

- Co-founder of River of Life Assemblies International (2002 to date)

- Visionary of Teens for Jesus, empowering and guiding teenagers in their walk with Jesus

- Founder of the Pastors' Wives Arise Network International (PWANI), empowering pastors' wives in their spiritual, family, and community roles. (2014 to date)

- Visionary of THE HOUR OF DECISION TV (THODtv), a Gospel broadcasting platform. (2016 to date)

- Visionary THE WARRIOR BRIDE HAS ARISEN Conferences (2022 to date)

Married to Bishop Dr. Israel Forlu for over forty-three years, Dr. Mercy Forlu is a devoted wife and mother to five children and ten grandchildren, all actively serving God. With a heart for counseling, she passionately assists those needing healing and restoration, guiding them toward purpose and fulfillment in Christ. As a sought-after conference speaker and empowerment advocate, Dr. Mercy Forlu continues to inspire and uplift countless individuals worldwide. To God be the glory.

Made in the USA
Middletown, DE
07 September 2024

59953829R00117